REMOVALS
SELECTION CARTAGE
SPRINGS
STOOR
VERPAK
HUISRAAD
SPOOR
3
20 M.P.H

ERF
Pat Kennett

WORLD TRUCKS NO 1

ts TRANSPORTATION SERIES

AZTEX CORPORATION
7002 E. PASEO SAN ANDRES
TUCSON, ARIZONA 85710

Also in the same series and by the same author
No 2 : Scania
No 3 : Seddon Atkinson
No 4 : MAN

© Patrick Stephens Limited 1978

All rights reserved. No part of this publication
may be reproduced, stored in a retrieval system,
or transmitted, in any form or by any means,
electronic, mechanical, photocopying,
recording or otherwise, without prior permission
in writing from Patrick Stephens Limited
or Aztex Corporation.

First published in 1978

Design by Tim McPhee

Printed in Great Britain
Library of Congress Catalog Card Number 78-53438
ISBN 0-89404-006-5

CONTENTS

SMALL BEGINNINGS   5

WAR AND PEACE   26

INNOVATION AND EXPANSION   43

SERVICE AND SUCCESS   80

AUTHOR'S PREFACE

In this book, the aim has not been to present a microscopically detailed catalogue or chronicle of everything that ERF made or did from the outset, for that would occupy a very large volume indeed. Instead I have tried to present an accurate outline sketch of the company's activities, its characters, its adventures and its products, from the dark post-depression days of the early 1930s up to the late 1970s, when equally severe, though different problems beset the commercial world. In so doing, it has been necessary to omit a great deal of fascinating detail contributed by my many friends, who willingly set about digging out forgotten facts and fables concerning ERF when they learned about this book. However, blending together all those snippets of information was a pleasant and absorbing task, almost akin to bringing history to life again, which indeed ERF have themselves done by restoring to perfection the first vehicle they ever built and which is illustrated on the cover of the book.

Particular thanks must go to Ernest Sherratt and Peter Foden for the time they devoted to my questions when they could have been far better employed looking after the thousand and one items of company business that directors need to attend to. To many ERF dealers and operators too, in particular Ken Beresford and Eric Baker, who spent a lot of time researching in their files for me, sincere thanks are due. It would be ungracious of me not to mention the tireless enthusiasm of Brian Tankard, ERF's public relations manager, in ensuring that no possible sources of information and illustrations were neglected. To those good friends, and all the others who helped the work along its way, all I can say is that I hope you obtain as much pleasure in reading the finished work as I did in producing it.

Pat Kennett

SMALL BEGINNINGS

The industrial and commercial slump in 1928-33 that afflicted Britain, indeed Europe and the United States too, was the cause of many basically sound vehicle manufacturers going out of business, never to be heard of again. In that context, the independent truck builders ERF Ltd, who are based at the little Cheshire market town of Sandbach in the northwest of England, are unique.

It was the depression that gave birth to the now famous ERF heavy truck. Starting from almost unbelievably humble beginnings, with four men huddled in the chilly confines of a borrowed greenhouse at Easter in 1933, that company has developed steadily and strongly over the years under the control of the same family that brought it into the world. The name of that family is familiar, Foden. The birth of the ERF lineage, and its connections with that original Foden company, present a closely entwined picture of engineering, commercial and human problems. In fact it has been said, with some justification, that the primary force in the emergence of the new company was the board policy of Fodens Ltd in the late 1920s, negative and unwitting contributors though they may have been.

The last years of the 1920s, a decade that had begun with a thriving commercial vehicle industry throughout the world following the lean war years, saw deepening problems in every sector of industry. A general slump was imminent, business confidence was waning fast and money was in increasingly short supply. Added to that there were internal troubles at Fodens Ltd. With one or two exceptions the members of the Foden family who had developed the firm through the first two decades of the century had given up the manufacturing industry and were farming in Australia. The company was under the general managership of one Mr Wood Whittle, and the chairman was Francis Poole. Senior Foden family man was Edwin Richard Foden, who was engineering director, while his son Dennis was a salesman with the company. Reluctant to abandon the steam wagons on which the company had made its reputation Fodens found many of their traditional customers going elsewhere to buy oil-engined lorries, as diesels were then called, which were much more efficient and easier to operate than steamers. Unconvinced, Wood Whittle ordered the building of a revolutionary steamer in 1930-31 which had pneumatic tyres just like the petrol and diesel engined trucks, with a high-speed poppet valve engine and an unusual all-welded boiler in place of the common rivetted type. The design was not a success and the gloom at Fodens deepened, accompanied by wholesale staff lay-offs, a high degree of redundancy and plummeting levels of orders. True, Fodens were beginning to build internal combustion-engined vehicles, but only in an exploratory fashion as the board still clung to the idea of steam. By 1930 they were building a trickle of relatively modern trucks alongside the remaining steamers.

It was against this troubled background that Edwin Richard Foden, approaching retirement after a life's work in transport, discussed the situation with his son Dennis. They were firmly of the opinion that the oil-engined truck was the way to go and that the steamer would soon be dead. His protests on the way things were going fell on deaf ears. So amid all manner of rumours E.R. Foden resigned from Fodens Ltd towards the end of 1932 and ostensibly retired.

However, that was far from being the last heard of him. Early in 1933, amid still more rumours, E.R. and Dennis Foden talked to George Faulkner, another resigned Foden manager related to them by marriage, and decided to form a team to examine the possibility of building their own oil-engined truck chassis. Both were keen steam men, but new legislation and the thoughts of operators favoured the 'oilers' and they were realistic enough to discipline themselves to the commercial world, personal enthusiasms notwithstanding. They enlisted the help of Ernest Sherratt, who with seven years experience in the workshops at Fodens, followed by a similar period in chassis design, was well versed in all aspects of automotive practice. On the Monday following Easter week in 1933 the four got together for the first time in their headquarters, a borrowed greenhouse at the rear of a house in Elworth near Sandbach belonging to E.R. Foden's eldest daughter. Between them they formed a simple policy which has remained with ERF to this day. That policy was to use the finest components that could be obtained to do the job required, and blend them together with a high degree of expertise and skill to form a vehicle of exceptional efficiency and durability.

That sounds very grand now, but to those four men in the greenhouse it was still a dream. The depression seemed to be continuing unabated in its fifth year. Few users were demanding trucks. Money was scarce. However, such was the confidence that component builders had in E.R. and his son Dennis, that such well known faces as Joe and Tom Gardner of Gardner engines, Fred Cowell of Kirkstall Axles, Frank Brown of David Brown and many others beat a regular path to the greenhouse door. And the four intrepid men toured the Northwest and Midlands in Dennis Foden's Alvis, visiting suppliers, potential users, and possible contributors as they planned their venture. Their enthusiasm came as a glimmer of light in the gloom of those times. Although the nominal capital of the new company, which had been named E.R. Foden and Son and made a limited company soon after its launch, was quite substantial at £20,000 (of which E.R. held £12,000 for himself) much of the supply of components was negotiated on a 'sale or return' basis. Nobody knew whether the venture would succeed, least of all the suppliers, and in that context the trust of those suppliers is indeed remarkable.

The whole environment in those early days was simple to the extent of being primitive. Ernest Sherratt got a pattern maker of his acquaintance to make him a drawing board on which he sketched out his first general arrangements and began to work in the details of his first chassis. The first working prints from those drawings were made by exposing the ferro-prussic sensitive paper in an old picture frame. Although the greenhouse was adequate—just—for a design and planning office, clearly it would not do to build truck chassis. As luck would have it the local coachbuilders J.H. Jennings had a vacant small workshop, previously occupied by a baby-linen firm who had moved to larger premises, and this warm and well-lit area was suitable. It was rented in June of that year as the design took shape and a small work force composed almost entirely of ex-Foden men began building the first chassis. There were only ten men all told at that stage, but such was the skill of the men involved, together with the enthusiasm of Dennis Foden himself, that the first vehicle was completed in August, less than six months after the first meeting in the greenhouse and was delivered to its owner on September 1. In order that the menfolk could concentrate on the task of creating their new lorry, Dennis' wife, Madge, did all the typing and paperwork in those first few critical months of the new company; but that was not all. Dennis decided that it would be great publicity if he could demonstrate how easy the new truck was to drive. Consequently, Madge Foden found herself driving the first truck out of their small workshop, and later she demonstrated the ERF to several customers.

Building chassis was one thing, selling them was something else. As it happened Ted Foden, who had been in Australia with the rest of the family, had returned to Britain and was working as a freelance salesman. He did a deal with ERF on the basis that he would collect £50 for some chassis he sold. He was as good as his word for even before the finishing touches were put to that first chassis Ted had found a buyer, Fred Gilbert, a haulier at Leighton Buzzard in Bedfordshire. There is a delightful story that soon after that Ted Foden sold a batch of ten chassis to the Stonehenge Brick Co, and the subsequent parting with £500 was the cause of a certain amount of pain to Dennis Foden who was not a man to throw his hard-earned cash about without good reason. Although Ted Foden was one of the contributors in getting ERF off the ground, he eventually rejoined Fodens Ltd when William Foden returned from Australia to become Managing Director of the company on the departure of Wood Whittle. But the sales score showed that this new maker in the tough world of truck building looked like being a success despite the hard times and the enormity of the task that faced them. The real secret of that success lay in the design of the vehicle itself. For its time it was an advanced, almost revolutionary design.

E.R. and Dennis Foden were quite clear in their brief; the new truck had to be simple and reliable, embodying the finest components available, while at the same time weight had to be kept low in order that payload could be kept high.

The then-new Gardner oil engine had been used in a few chassis at Fodens with good results, so one of the first major decisions was to fit Gardner engines. In fact every ERF built up to the war years, when supply dictates changed things, was fitted with a Gardner engine, and again after the war Gardner was the standard power unit for many years. The four cylinder 4LW type engine was chosen for the prototype, to which a David Brown four-speed gear-

SMALL BEGINNINGS

box was mounted as a single unitised assembly. That in itself was unusual as most trucks other than the light one- or two-tonners had their gearboxes mounted as separate units with a shaft from the engine.

In the early 1930s, the Kirkstall Forge company had developed a range of industrial axles, both driving and steering types, and after careful examination these were approved by the team from Sandbach and included in the design. A simple ladder type frame was designed with its width dictated by the requirement that the springs should be underneath the frame sidemembers where the loads would not tend to twist the structure. Crossmembers and spring brackets were added using the most positive method known at that time which was fitted bolting. That meant that every part had the holes reamed to a very accurate size when actually in position on the frame and the bolts were a tight fit in those holes. That gave a very strong frame assembly with minimum weight.

Brakes were the then-new vacuum hydraulic type, with hydraulic circuits to all wheels, aided by a large vacuum servo unit mounted on the right-hand sidemember between the axles. The system broke new ground in truck braking and the ERF had the best brakes in the business. Lockheed supplied the hydraulics, Clayton Dewandre the servos. A single piece propeller shaft with oil-immersed universal joints took the drive to the rear axle and it passed through the centre of the crossmember which lay ahead of the axle. This 'banjo' crossmember was an ERF hallmark for many years, as were the spring hangers, which were basically unchanged until well after the Second World War. Some parts have lived even longer. For example the shackle pins on that first design were part number 10. And on today's ERFs the shackle pin is still part number 10. The material is improved and they are plated now, but the original design remains.

E.R. and Dennis insisted that their new truck should offer an unprecedented degree of comfort and protection for the driver, and at the same time give a modern and up-to-date appearance. How well they succeeded can be seen from the photographs. That cab looked years ahead of all its competitors in 1933, and 15 years later when the basic shape was finally discarded it was by no means an obsolete looking structure. J.H. Jennings built the cabs for the Fodens Father and Son, using a light timber frame with a wooden floor, and aluminium panels. The rear bulkhead panel was made of fibreboard — what we would call hardboard today — and though that brought a number of complaints from users, the same material was retained in the interests of light weight for at least ten years. That was a far cry from the cabs of the 1970s which have to withstand enormous shock loads and impacts in order to meet international legislation.

Just how well the design work had been done is confirmed by the speed at which that first chassis was completed, and delivered to its owner on September 1. Outside the little team at Sandbach, very few people really believed that an advanced new truck was in the making, and sceptics prophesied failure at every turn. But they were wrong. Before the first chassis was delivered and given the number 63, to mark the age of E.R. Foden at the time, three further chassis were started. With full co-operation of the component suppliers, who it will be remembered had provided the original materials on a sale or return basis and were delighted that the product had been sold so quickly, numbers 64, 65 and 66 were laid down and all were completed within six weeks of the first chassis being delivered. Things were moving and confidence that had been confined to the original team spread rapidly to everyone involved.

In those days the London Show was held at Olympia and a stand space was hurriedly booked for the exhibition to be held in November. Chassis 65 was earmarked as a show exhibit although it had been sold to a firm in Harpenden, A. Saunders and Son. Numbers 64 and 66 had already been delivered to their owners, so two of the next three chassis were also earmarked for the Olympia show. They were numbers 68 and 69, sold respectively to George Baker, a Southampton haulier whose family still operates ERFs today, and to J. Egerton Quested of Cheriton, Kent.

Those three trucks were arguably the stars of the 1933 show. They were designed for operation at 12 tons gross and with weights of under four tons complete with bodywork, hauliers saw in them a thoroughly profitable vehicle. In fact the trucks were sold as being able to carry six tons, but overloading was the rule rather than the exception and it is doubtful if those early ERFs ever ran with less than eight tons aboard. While the show was in progress the first dealer agreements were made with J. Bowen and Sons of Musselborough in Scotland and with W.J. Boyes and Son of Peckham in south-east London. There was tremendous enthusiasm among dealers and the new users alike and by the end of the year there was a very healthy forward order situation which, in times still affected by the aftermath of the slump, was more than E.R. and Dennis had dared hope. By the end of the year a more powerful version had been built in reply to those hauliers who wanted to pull a trailer and found the little 4LW Gardner a bit breathless for such loads. Gardner suggested their 5LW engine and though five cylinders were very unusual in motor vehicles the move was an instant success. Low speed pulling torque was particularly good with the 5LW and as the year 1934 got under way there were steady streams of orders for the more powerful truck which was known simply as the CI5.

In the first year of operation, including the five-months design period, 31 trucks were built. The following year that figure was more than trebled to 96 trucks, and almost doubled again to 175 in 1935-6. All that was achieved by adhering rigidly to the original concept of a simple, reliable but high quality vehicle.

There was no doubt that in the new ERFs operators had found a remarkably effective vehicle. The owner of the very first one, Fred Gilbert, reported some months later that he expected, and got, a fuel consumption fully loaded around the 20 miles per gallon mark, or 14 litres per 100 kilometres, which is very good economy indeed for a 12 ton truck, even by today's standards. Not only were they economical, but they were extraordinarily durable too. Just how durable is illustrated by the history of chassis number 137, built in May 1934 for George Baker, who had bought one of the Olympia show chassis the previous November. That truck worked solidly right through into the 1950s when it was rebuilt as a tractive unit and re-registered. Then in its new guise it worked on, right through the 1960s and finally was scrapped in 1970 after 37 years of work when the teeth of the 1968 Transport Act really began to bite. Even in today's environment of tight technical and legislative standards Britain's highways are regularly travelled by ERFs that are 20 years old or more.

Happy though they were with the four-wheeled CI4 and 5 chassis, dealers were pressing for the bigger, heavier trucks that were being demanded by the operators. So in the summer of 1934 design work was started on heavy duty three-axled and four-axled chassis. The three-axle type was laid down first, as a tandem-drive six wheeler, but in fact the eight wheeler was the first to be completed just before Christmas 1934. The six wheeler did not appear until well into January 1935, but both were as successful as the original four wheelers had been. The multi-axle chassis were usually powered by the 6LW Gardner engine which used identical parts to the four and five cylinder engines and developed 103 horsepower. However, some were built with five cylinder engines, in which case they were usually single drive machines. Most six cylinder types had tandem drive rear bogies. The introduction of these bigger chassis led to more complex type numbers. The six cylinder engine models were called naturally, CI6s, with an additional number denoting six or eight wheels and yet another number denoting single or tandem axle drive. So a CI6-62 was a six wheeler with tandem axle drive and the Gardner 6LW engine. These bigger chassis also used the David Brown four-speed gearbox, which still had many years of life ahead of it, though the five-speed box was often fitted to multiwheelers.

Although some users were requiring bigger and bigger trucks, others wanted lighter machines, and even though the four cylinder ERF was among the lightest of its class available it was thought that a combination of the quality of the normal ERF and the low weight of some of the petrol-engined chassis then on the market would be a feasible proposition. So a new chassis was built, following the same basic concept again, but utilising a much lighter frame and axles and a Gardner 3LW three cylinder engine. Without its cab this model weighed under two tons and many were built and fully bodied at under three tons, to operate at seven tons gross. However, acceptance of the three cylinder engine was not over enthusiastic and eventually the model which had been called the OE3 was changed to include the very light 3.8 litre four cylinder 4LK Gardner. This was much smoother and quieter than the 3LW and the model immediately became very popular indeed. There were a few lightweight normal chassis known as 2C14s but they were outclassed by the really light OE.

Later on the type became known as the LK series rather than by its original OE label, but the design remained unchanged, continuing that rigid, basic concept laid down in 1933. The first OE lightweights appeared in 1934 and the 4LK-powered version in the summer of 1937, but it was still the traditional CI4, 5 and 6 chassis that formed the bulk of production. In the years immediately before the Second World War ERF had become one of Britain's major truck builders, turning out well over 400 trucks a year and that dream of Easter 1933 had become a very solid reality indeed.

SMALL BEGINNINGS

Right Edwin Richard Foden and **far right** Dennis Foden, the founders.

Below This is where it all began. On the 21st anniversary of the company, Ernest Sherratt (left) Dennis Foden and George Faulkner (right) revisited the greenhouse in Elworth near Sandbach where they and E.R. Foden formulated their plans and designed the first ERF.

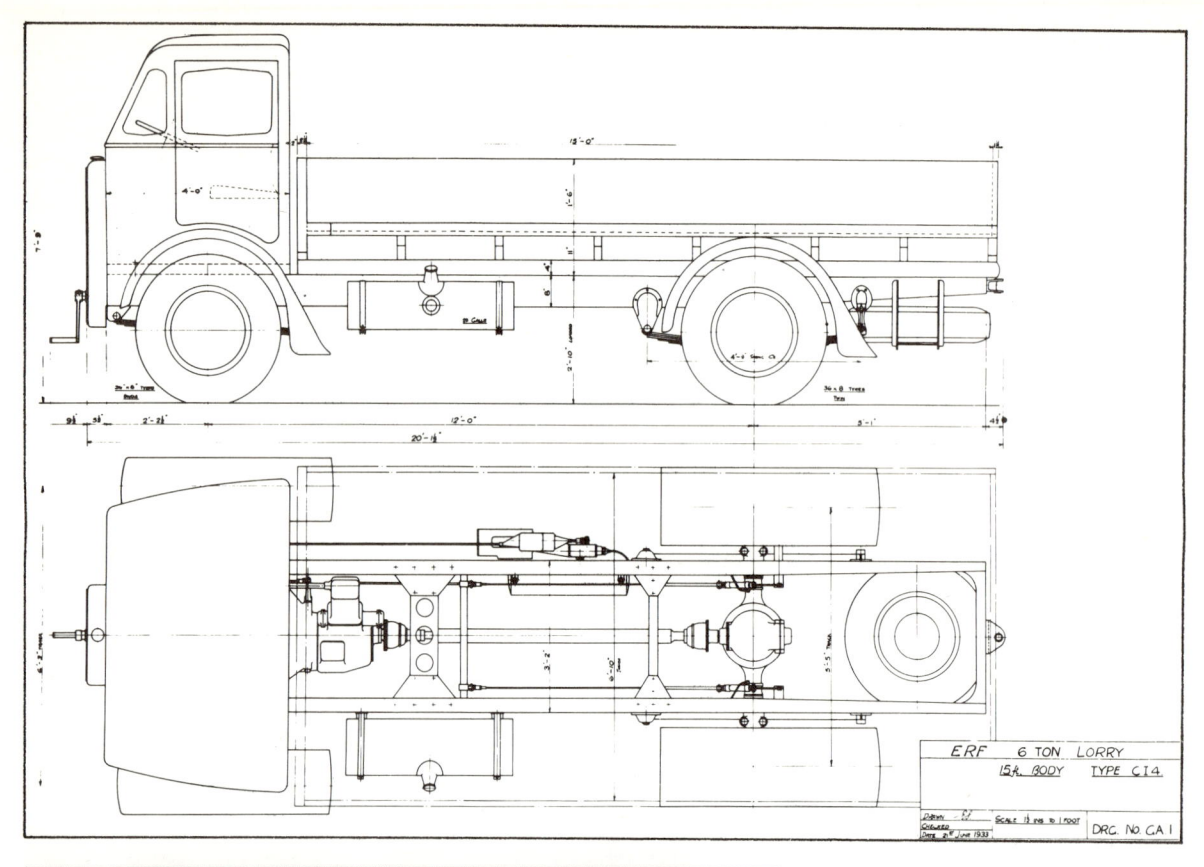

Above How it all started. This is the general arrangement drawing of the original ERF. For its time it was very advanced. For example vacuum servo brakes, a wide frame with the springs directly underneath it, and a good looking fully enclosed cab made it extremely attractive to operators. Its low weight and outstanding fuel economy backed up that attraction in everyday service.

Left The first chassis had the legend 'E.R. Foden & Son' on the radiators, but this was changed to ERF after the 1933 motor show, at the request of neighbouring Fodens Ltd. This is the first ERF, given chassis number 63, which was E.R. Foden's age at the time.

SMALL BEGINNINGS

Right No secret was made of ERF's Foden background in the early days. This explanation appeared in one of the earliest catalogues.

Captions for photos on the following two pages

Page 12, top Costing list in 1933, used in working out the chassis price contains some astonishing items. £3.11 shillings and 6 pence for a pair of springs and 12 shillings and 6 pence for a silencer sound like good bargains.

Page 12, bottom The prototype 1933 ERF was an immediate success, due to its high quality, low weight, very modern appearance and its promise of long reliable service. Ever since then, ERFs have never strayed far from that basic formula.

Page 13, top One of the earliest dealers was W.J. Boyes and Son, then at Peckham, now based at Grays. Early in 1934 they had this truck built as a demonstrator and succeeded in producing a steady stream of orders. This was chassis number 120, a standard CI5 with a 15 foot body. Although most chassis before that had ERF on the radiator this one somehow emerged with the original 'E.R. Foden & Son' badge.

Page 13, bottom Scant details of the early vehicles were entered in the chassis record book. Clearly the staff were more concerned with getting the details right on the actual vehicles.

WHAT IS BEHIND AN E.R.F.?
By E. R. FODEN.

My first connection with Transport was in the year 1878, when I was only eight years old, driving a Traction Engine belonging to my late father Edwin Foden. In 1880, the first Traction Engine to be built in Sandbach had many of my ideas incorporated in it. I designed the first steam wagon on steel tyres in 1898, which had a long run until the year 1913, then I fitted the solid rubber tyres which were very successful until the year 1928. I then fitted the first steam wagon on pneumatic tyres, and these wagons had a run until 1931, as steam appeared to be going out of favour with transport users in this year I designed a 6/8 ton chassis to take the famous Gardner Oil Engine and its success prompted me to contemplate building a 4/6 ton Diesel Wagon.

In July 1932 my plans were interrupted by my decision to retire, thinking I had deserved a well earned rest. After being in retirement for some time I had many requests from my old customers and friends to go into business again. In the meantime recent legislation has decided that the maximum load carrying capacity wagon to sell in any quantity must have an unladen weight of under 4 tons. Therefore my son and I have decided to manufacture a vehicle in this taxation class and have included in this weight the strongest frame, the most powerful engine, a robust gear box and sturdy axles coupled with efficient and powerful brakes. We are building this vehicle on totally different business methods which we know will reduce very considerably overhead charges and in that way our customers will reap the benefit.

It will give us great pleasure and be much to your interest to let us quote you the next time you are buying Commercial Vehicles.

PARTS.	ESTIMATED PRICES.			REVISED.			FINAL.		
	£	S	D	£	S	D	£	S	D
Front Axle.	41	10	0	41	10	0	41	10	0
Rear Axle.	98	10	0	98	10	0	98	10	0
Axle Bolts and Plates.	0	0	0	0	0	0			
Steering Box	12	0	0	12	0	0	12	0	0
Drop Arm and Ball.	0	0	0						
Tyres. 36 x 8.	51	16	0	51	16	0	51	16	0
Seven Wheels.	11	9	0	11	7	11	10	4	0
Gear Box & Change Speed.	65	0	0	65	0	0	65	0	0
Speedometer Drive.	0	0	0	0	0	0			
Front Springs. (2)	2	19	0	3	9	0	3	11	6
Rear Springs. (2).	4	18	6	4	14	0	4	14	6
Spring Packing Plates.	0	0	0	0	4	6		4	6
1 - Set of Spring Brackets.	4	0	0	5	14	6	5	14	6
Spicer Shaft.	12	15	0	7	15	0	7	15	0
Companion Flanges. (2).	3	0	0	0	0	0			
Bolts & Nuts.	1	0	0				1	0	0
Spring Bracket Bushes.		9	0	0	4	6		4	6
Radiator.	14	0	0	14	0	0	14	0	0
Radiator Brackets.	1	10	0	0	0	0			
Lighting Set.	12	0	0	13	8	6	13	8	6
Dashboard.	2	0	0						
Wires.	1	0	0				1	0	0
Fuel Tank	4	0	0					18	6
Fuel Tank Brackets.	0	0	0	1	10	0			
Fuel Tank Bands.	0	0	0	0	7	6	0	7	6
Fuel Tank Gauge.	0	0	0		10	6		10	6
Servo Cylinder Clayton.	7	8	3	7	8	3	7	8	3
Lockheed Cyls. (piping).	8	11	9				8	11	9
Hand Brake & Fittings.	5	0	0				5	0	0
Frame. & Bolts.	11	10	0	9	10	0	9	10	0
Shackles. (8)	0	0	0	1	0	0	1	0	0
Engine Brackets.	4	0	0	5	5	0	3	17	0
1-Set of Shackle Pins.	1	17	8	0	19	4	18	11	
Silencer.	3	10	0	1	3	0	12	6	
Silencer Piping 6ft.		19	0		12	6	12	6	
Drag Link & Pins.	2	7	6	2	2	0			
	3	0	0		13	3	13	3	
	6	0	0				6	0	0
	3	0	0	1	17	6	1	17	6
	4	0	0				4	0	0
	314	8	0	300	0	0	300	0	0
	11	12	0	11	12	0	11	12	0
	4	0	0	4	0	0	4	0	0
	3	15	0	3	15	0			
	3	10	0						

Chassis No 63
Engine No 4LW 30510
Type CI 4
Rear Axle Ratio 28 : 1

Index No BLG 2711

7¼" Camber Rear Springs   5½" Centre Rear Shackles

Tyres Michelin Zig Zag 36 × 8

Bayo intermediate Crownwheel

AC Fuel Pump on Engine.

Engine No 52U 30424
Conversion

Purchaser :— W.F Gilbert
46 Bassett Road
Leighton Buzzard, Beds

Date of Delivery 1st Sept 1933

Norman Sandiway Transport
Sandiway

Date of Delivery June 7th 1933.

Left Heart of the original design was the 4LW Gardner oil engine. The five and six-cylinder versions in the later heavier models all incorporating interchangable moving parts.

Right Greater detail was recorded in the chassis record books as time went on, including details of signwriting and painting. Trade-in details were included in the costings, and it is interesting to note a number of Mercedes-Benz trade-in deals as early as 1934.

Below Since being restored, the original ERF has appeared at many historic vehicle rallies. Here it heads for Brighton in the rain on the HCVC Brighton Run in 1973.

Chassis no. 133   Date of Order
                   June 20th 1934

J. Highfield

Type: C.T.S. 7ton Standard.   Engine No. 5LW/31754.) Bosch [...]
Engine: Gardner 5 cyl. 5 LW type.
Gearbox: Four speeds. Rear axle ratio 6.25:1.
Wheelbase: 13' 6".
Tyres: 36" x 8" Michelin.
Brakes: Lockheed on all four wheels. Handbrake on rear wheels.
           "Mole" trailer brake control.

Fuel Tank: 32 gal. capacity.
Stg. gear: Fitted with Haworth joints.
Cab: Saloon pattern. Front pulling jaw required.
Body: 17'6" x 6'11" wide. Flush platform. Hinged & divided [...]
           panel sides 1'6" deep. Tailboard same height as cab top.
           Tailboard 1'6" deep. Detachable cratch extensions same height
           as footboard. Two slag bars to cratches.

Lamps: 12 volt. bride battery. Side lamps attached to cab sides. [...]
Colour: Body & cab all yellow to sample (N/1003). Chassis & mudguards
           Black. Wheels Yellow.

Lettering: In Black, shaded Red.
                                    BURTON TRANSPORT   LONDON AGENTS
                                         PHONE 3165   HERBERT GRANT & SON
                                                            C. Lloyds Avenue
           On cab sides:-   BURTON-ON-TRENT   LONDON, E.C.3
                                                                 ALSO
                                                            LONDON WALL 0311
                                     BURTON TRANSPORT   (4 LINES)

           On cab front:-   ┌─BURTON─┐
                                     │SERVICE │   ⊙
                                     └TRANSPORT┘

           On sideboards (near side):- YOU'LL BAKE REALLY WELL ON A "BAKEWELL" oven
                        (off side):- TO BAKE WELL USE A "BAKEWELL" GRATE

           On tailboard:-   BAKEWELL GRATES
                                      ARE MADE AT
                                      BURTON-ON-TRENT

Regn: Appn. form to C.C.C.   Regn. No. BLG 799.
           U.W. 3T. 1c. 3q. (without cratches)   Wt. tkt. to C.C.C. 21/7/34.

Price: 1375. 0. 0   On H.P. terms arranged with
             10. 0. 0 extra for long platform   Wray & Co. (W) Ltd.
             12. 0. 0   " " trailer brake control.
             15. 15. 0   " " self-starter.   1375. 0. 0
              5. 6. 0   " " bride battery.   25% deposit 343. 15. 0
              8. 0. 0   " " cratches.   1031. 5. 0
           1426. 0. 0   15% interest 134. 1. 3
            206. 5. 0 15% discount off list price (£1375)   £1165. 6. 3 payable by
           £1219. 15. 0   24 monthly instalments of £48.11.1
                                                    All payments guaranteed by
Extras: Wakefield's (oil) notified 16/7/34.   E.R. Foster & Son.
                                                    (Extras charged separately)

SCOTTS
BAMPTON
SCOTTS
BAMPTON
SCOTTS
JOHN KIRKLAND
DERBY
ERF

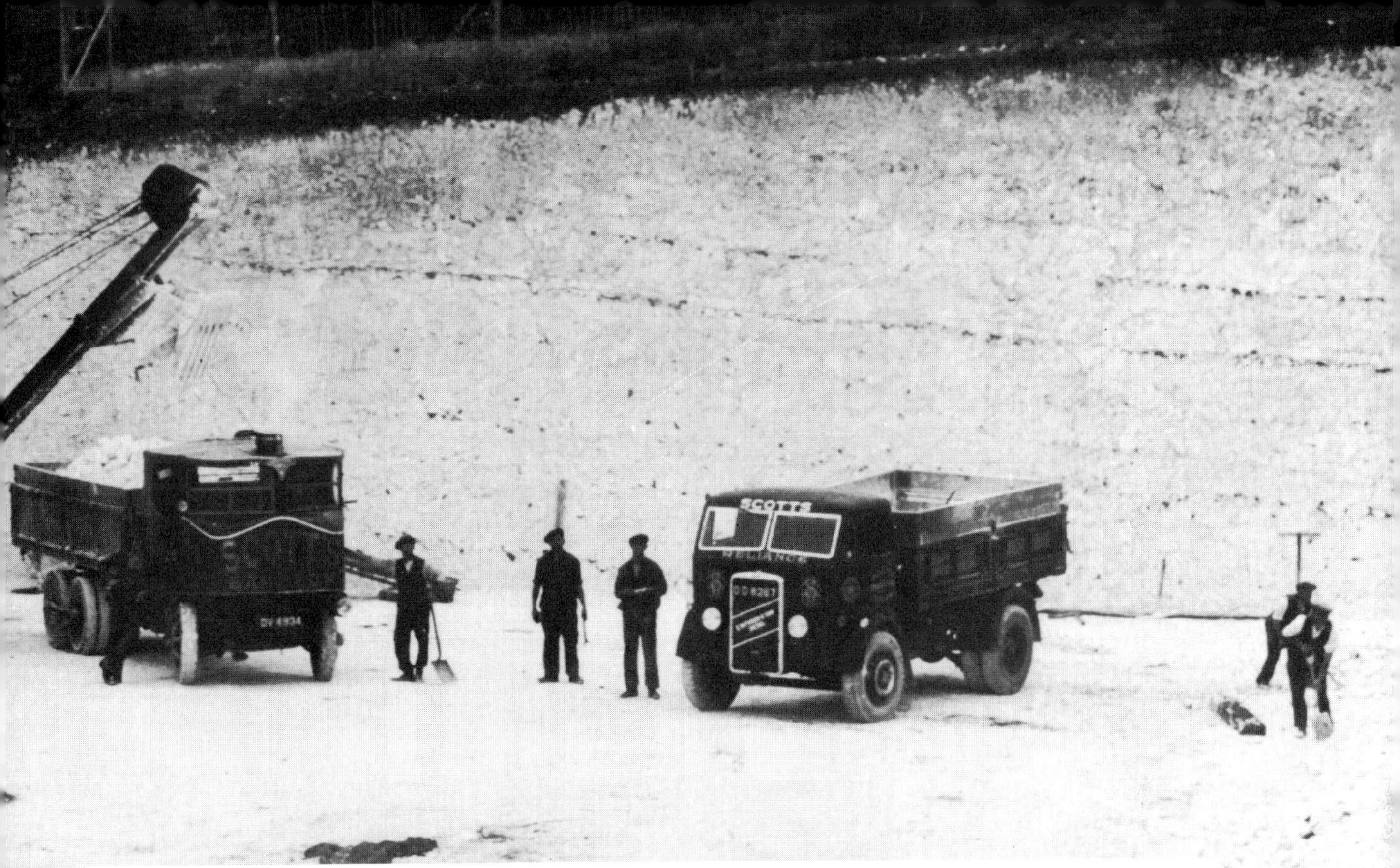
SCOTTS
DV 6934

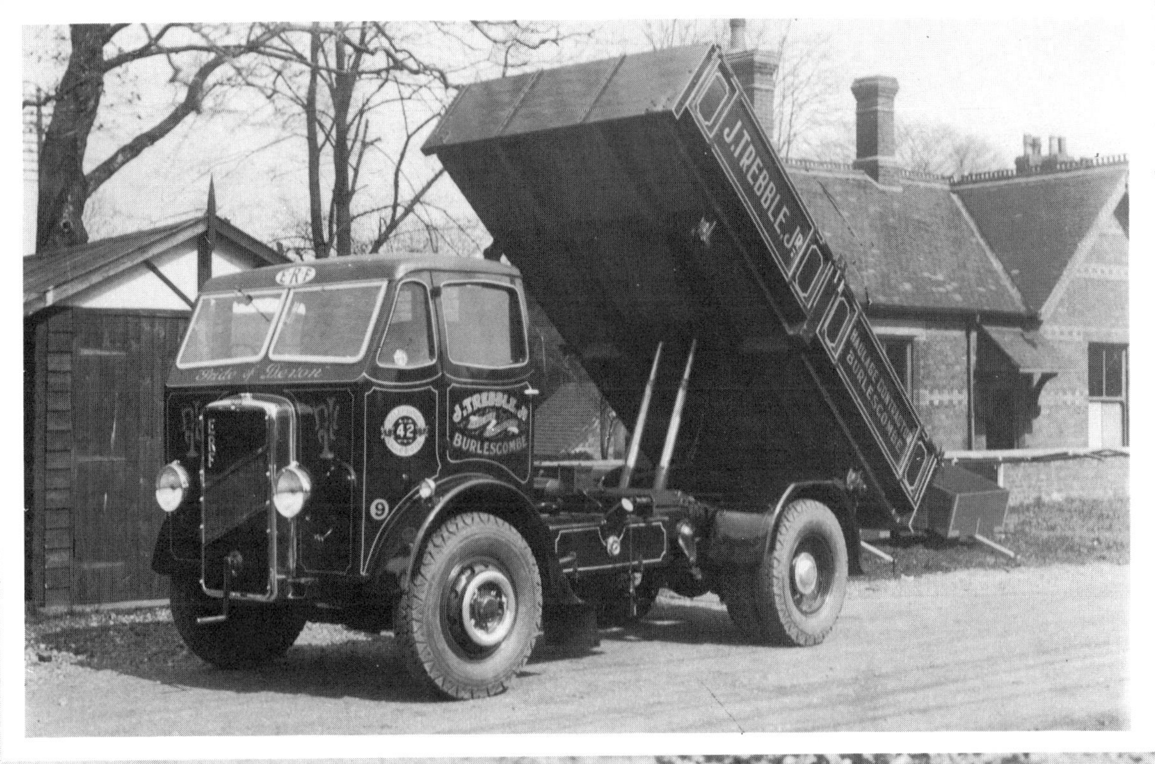
ERF
J. TREBBLE, Jr
BURLESCOMBE

Photographs on the previous two pages:

Background Construction of a new reservoir in the downs behind Brighton in 1934 involved three Sentinel steam wagons—two six wheelers on solid tyres—an ancient Ruston shovel and a brand new ERF, all owned by Devonshire construction contractors, Scotts.

Left inset Tractive units were added to the catalogue from 1935. This is an early example built for John Kirkland, later to become part of the specialist heavy haulage concern of Bowmer and Kirkland. Like the heavier rigid trucks, the tractive units had Gardner 5LW engines.

Right inset A three-way tipping body was offered ex-works from March 1934 and this proved very popular during the road-building boom in Britain during the late 1930s. The chassis had changed little from the prototype, though for a while the ERF letters were mounted in the top corner of the radiator.

Right This page from the 1934 show catalogue shows several interesting points. It illustrates the contrived testimonial means of advertising, which even though undoubtedly true would not be very convincing today. It also shows the fashion of having a picture of a truck on hauliers' letterheads. Note also that in 1934 horse and steam haulage is quoted.

Below left and below By 1935 heavy six wheelers were in full production, offering an alternative to the two axle types. The first chassis, built in January, had 'balloon' rear tyres on 13.5 x 20 section and was the first ERF design to use the 6LW Gardner engine. Following the existing type number system it was called the CI6-6. With body it weighed under 6 tons. Some six wheelers were built with five-cylinder engines.

Bottom Although a later chassis number than the first six wheeler, the first rigid eight was in fact completed six weeks earlier just before Christmas 1934. Called the CI6-8 and with 103 horsepower the big ERF was probably the most powerful and advanced heavy truck available in UK at that time.

SMALL BEGINNINGS

A Typical Testimonial

Mr. W. F. Gilbert,
96, Bassett Road,
Leighton Buzzard, Beds., *says:—*

ERF

"With a 7-ton load I average 20 m.p.g. I do quite a lot of driving myself and can assure you that I enjoy driving my 'E.R.F.' quite as well as my pleasure car."

Telegrams: TUCKWELL, OXFORD.

Telephone: No. 2143 OXFORD (Private Line).
46 EYNSHAM (Cassington Pit).

FROM

H. Tuckwell & Sons, Ltd.,

Builders' Merchants, Contracting Carmen, etc.,

128 BULLINGDON ROAD, OXFORD

(Branch Office: L.M. & S. Ry. Station).

SAND, BALLAST AND LOAM SUPPLIED TO ORDER.

Estimates Given for Carting by the Hour, Day or Week,
by Horses, Steam, or Petrol Power.

TERMS: MONTHLY NET.

DIRECTORS:
H. W. TUCKWELL, GOVERNING DIRECTOR.
E. M. TUCKWELL.
W. B. TUCKWELL.
A. J. TUCKWELL.
J. B. TUCKWELL.
G. K. TUCKWELL.
D. M. TUCKWELL, SECRETARY.

GET/RP

March 31st, 1934

Messrs. E.R. Foden & Son.,
Sun Works,
Sandbach,
CHESHIRE.

Dear Sirs,

    With reference to the E.R.F. Diesel Lorries we have purchased from you. These vehicles are giving complete satisfaction and the fact that we have ordered five of them three being repeat orders is adequate proof of the excellent results being obtained.

    The easy manner in which they can be manoeuvred in awkward places and their ability to withstand really hard work without mechanical trouble is a great asset.

    The finely built chassis and cab, with excellent brakes, steering and controls coupled with the famous Gardner Engines which are very reliable and extremely economical with fuel, make these vehicles in our opinion the best proposition on the road.

Yours faithfully,
H. TUCKWELL & SONS LTD

G. E. Tuckwell Secretary

from a purchaser of FIVE E.R.F. lorries

Left The first Tasker low-loader to be built with giant pneumatic tyres instead of solids was operated behind a CI5 ERF by George Baker, Southampton.

Below Many of the CI5 models in the 1930s operated with trailers like this one operated by Beresford Caddy and Pemberton in 1937. For such work they were usually fitted with a 6.25 axle ratio and later versions had a five speed gear box.

SMALL BEGINNINGS

Right The CI6-8 developed into a popular heavy duty tipper and many of them were built during 1935-36-37. Since that time rigid 'eights' have always featured prominently in the ERF catalogue.

Below right Even in the mid-1930s Sun Works was an imposing sight, though quite small in ground area. The weather vane is interesting. The site was expanded in area almost annually throughout the 1930s.

F.E.KING
F.E.KING & Co. LTD
ROAD TRANSPORT CONTRACTORS
BRISTOL & LONDON
ERF

SIMPSON'S
T. SIMPSON & Co. (LEICESTER) LTD
T. SIMPSON & Co. (LEICESTER) LTD
BRIDGE HOUSE,
THE NEWARKE,
LEICESTER
PHONES
65148-9
ERF
LBC 548

SMALL BEGINNINGS   23

Left Although the standard ERF chassis and cab was very light, that was not enough for some. This parcels operator had a special lightweight cab and body built by Duramin on the four cylinder LK type chassis in 1938. The whole vehicle weighed well under three tons.

Right Cab interiors in the 1930s were considerably less attractive than the exteriors. Apart from seat upholstery there is no trim and it is a very long reach to the central switch and dash panel. There were no cab heaters either.

Below left The OE4 type, later known as the LK4 was extremely light for a diesel truck. This one, even with body and hydraulic tipping gear only weighed a fraction over three tons ready for the road.

Below The 4LK 3.8 litre Gardner engine was a highly successful unit in lightweight ERF models for well over 20 years, and many are still running today.

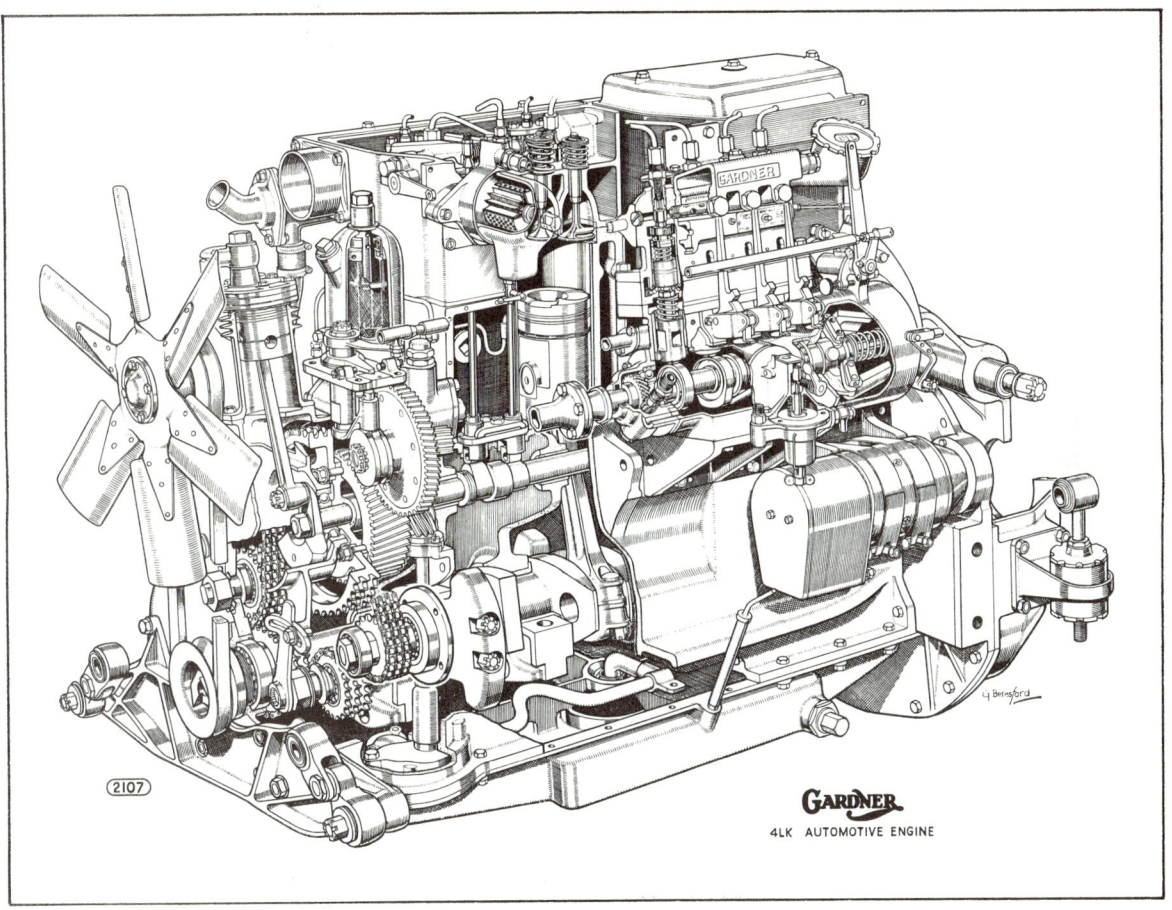

S. GRIMSHAW & SON
S. GRIMSHAW & SON
LEEDS
&
LONDON
LEEDS — LONDON · DAILY SERVICE

ERF
FTD 533

SMALL BEGINNINGS

Right Modesty was not among the attributes of ERF if the 1935 catalogue is any guide.

Left The first twin steer chassis—nicknamed the 'Chinese-six' by truck men—was built for a Yorkshire haulier in 1938. It was basically a CI5 chassis with a second steering axle, but the type never became popular in the pre-power-steering days. At that time the ERF letters were fastened to the upper corner of the grille.

Below left Elaborate special cab and body built on a CI5 chassis in 1938 for engine manufacturers, L. Gardner & Sons, Ltd. Signwriting on the cab is virtually a replica of the company's stationery.

Below Only one half-cab ERF was built. It looks suitable for bus bodywork but was in fact built to carry long steel bars.

THE WORLD'S BEST LORRY-

E·R·F

WAR AND PEACE

When war was declared in September 1939, ERF had yet to celebrate the sixth birthday of the production of their first chassis. In comparison with many other vehicle builders they were very much the new boys. But despite their 'junior' position in terms of years, their reputation as makers of top quality trucks was already a byword in the industry. Consequently, when decisions had to be taken about who would make what with the rapidly dwindling supplies of strategic raw materials, ERF got the go-ahead to continue truck production at a rate that was very little different from their peacetime volume. That meant that over 400 chassis a year were planned, and when the scarcity of diesel engines was taken into account, that is an astonishing figure. There were big differences though.

To begin with production was to continue with Gardner engines, mainly 4LW and 5LW models, as the bigger types were earmarked for use in tanks and other fighting vehicles. But even those grew scarce as more and more demands were made on the Patricroft firm, so for the first time other engines were put into ERFs. AEC 7.7 litre diesel engines, similar to those fitted in the famous Matador gun tractors, were the main choice, while Perkins engines — much higher-revving and lighter duty units than the Gardner engines — were also considered, though few were actually made. All this was done under the close watch of the Ministry of War Transport. They decided what would be built and for whom. More or less standard CI4 and CI5 trucks were built for the War Office, most of which joined the Royal Army Service Corps which was the army's transport wing, and large numbers of them were used in the Normandy landings to carry the vital supplies up to the front lines.

Meanwhile, the home war effort had to continue, and it could not do so without transport, so trucks were also built for civil users. In design these were identical to the prewar types except for substitution of engines in many cases — you were indeed lucky if you managed to get a Gardner-engined truck in those times. Radiators were painted instead of chromed and strict limits were placed on the type of bodies that could be built. There was to be no multi-curved panelling for example, that absorbed too much skilled labour, so bodies were very straight and square. Very small lamps were fitted too, as 'blackout' regulations were in force, and in most cases cowls were fitted over the lamps to reduce their visibility from the air. Other simplifications were introduced, like windows that lifted by hand rather than by a handle mechanism, but the basic chassis design was still like the pre-war machines.

As the war continued supplies of materials got more and more difficult and the numbers of chassis built dwindled steadily until, by 1944-5, it was under the 250-a-year mark. In fact it was not until well after the war, in 1953 after steel rationing had been finally done away with, that ERF's production got back to its prewar level. Just as the ERF had made a name for itself in peacetime as a tough truck, so it maintained that reputation at war, and many a tale has been told of their extraordinary durability. One such tale concerns an RASC unit in France which was working very close to the front when one of their already somewhat battered ERFs ran over a mine. The vehicle was blown into a field, the body wrenched off the chassis and its contents strewn far and wide. The sump was holed and the tyres were shredded. Its crew dragged it back on the roadside, somehow managed to get the remains of the body back on board again, patched the sump, pinched some tyres from a more badly damaged truck, collected up what they could find of their cargo, which was rations for the fighting troops, and went on their way delayed by only about five hours. That these men and trucks were officially classified as 'non-fighting' does not seem to have occurred to them as unusual!

Another ERF war tale concerns the initial stages of

preparation for seaborne landings in the dark days of 1942 when things were not going well for the Allied forces. Engineers from the War Office directed the preparation of an ERF for deep water wading and together with a truck of another make — not too far to the north — trials were held at the deserted seaside resort of Southport. Side by side the two trucks drove courageously out to sea amid cheers and 'God bless those who sail in her' remarks from those left ashore who had worked on them. There were not quite so many cheers 15 minutes later though when it was time to quit the watery deep. Only one truck emerged from the Irish sea that day and it was the ERF. Gardner were, of course, practised marine engine builders, but it is doubtful if that was what they had in mind!

The spirit of those at home during those sombre war years is well illustrated by the company's scheme to buy a Spitfire fighter and present it to the Royal Air Force. The going price for a Spitfire was apparently £5000 which seems extraordinarily cheap nearly 40 years afterwards. The big problem was how to raise that amount of money. Just whose idea it was is not recorded, but it was decided to run a raffle. No ordinary raffle this, but one with an ERF truck as first prize. At that time a new truck was an exceedingly scarce commodity and nobody seems to have dared to record how they managed to sell the idea to the Ministry of War Transport who controlled such things with unyielding severity. However, a truck was obtained, a lightweight LK long wheelbase type and the raffle commenced. Dealers, operators, workers and friends and families all chipped in, some buying a whole ticket, others sharing the £5 cost. In a matter of two or three weeks the £5000 was raised and a cheque sent to Lieutenant Colonel Moore-Brabazon who was Minister of Aircraft Production, together with a letter asking that a Spitfire be called 'ERF'. It was eventually called 'Sun Works' and went into squadron service with a Canadian unit of the RAF. All that took place in 1941 and it was to be four long years before the war clouds finally rolled away and thoughts could be turned once again to building trucks for industry and commerce on a full time basis.

After the war ceased, any thoughts that everything would be easy and prosperous were soon dispelled. True there was a demand for trucks from industry starved of transport for nearly six years. But finances were tight and raw materials were scarce and would remain so for several years, but perhaps worst of all there was a grave lack of skills available because the menfolk had either not returned from the war, or had returned having lost the skills they possessed before going off to fight. Things looked depressing after the long years of hope during hostilities. Playing safe, the ERF board decided that they could do no better than continue with their same basic design, updated with new accessories and equipment that were then becoming available. So the first postwar ERFs were almost identical to the prewar designs, though most had five and six cylinder engines, and very few four cylinder models were built except for the light LK models. The cab had gradually changed shape over the years, taking on a little more rake here, an extra curve there, but the severely uncompromising vertical radiator remained.

It was at this time that Peter Foden joined the company as an apprentice, working in the factory and the drawing offices and going to evening classes at technical college. By then ERF itself was larger than Jennings, and the imposing factory premises called Sun Works by E.R., who had a conviction that the sun was the source of most if not all things good on this earth, was a big plant by contemporary standards having been extended and rebuilt on several occasions. That factory needed a very appreciable volume of work to maintain it in profit, and that was hard to find in the lean postwar years.

The first major move to break out of this postwar depression was the decision to adopt a stylish new cab and radiator and couple that with an improved chassis. The first truck to the new design appeared in the spring of 1948 after several months of careful design work by Ernest Sherratt and his now sizable team. Although the chassis was still very much in the ERF style, it was stronger, had bigger and better brakes and it was more versatile. An extremely elegant curved radiator grille was incorporated which was to stay for ten years, and the standard chassis was turned out not with a complete cab, but with a curved dash plate which reflected the line of the radiator. A cab could be built on to this dash plate, as indeed many were before the chassis left the works. Alternatively, coachbuilders could erect stylish bodywork based on that same dash plate with the cab as an integral part of the body. Many remarkably elegant trucks were built using this principle and the new appearance marked an upturn in the fortunes of the company. A few steel cabs with pressings common to the Morris cab were used, but they were not markedly successful. Of course, Dennis Foden had a hand in the styling of the new cab, as indeed he had with the original. The standard cab was still a coach-built affair with a timber frame and floor and aluminium panelling, but the fibre board bulkhead at last disappeared.

Steel supplies were still on government allocation — there was no such thing as a free market — but because ERF had successfully pursued their export markets as soon as the war finished, they were assured of a regular if not abundant supply of materials. The Gardner engine was still the only type fitted, although others had been used during the war, and David Brown, Kirkstall and Lockheed still figured prominently in the chassis components suppliers lists.

In 1950 Edwin Richard Foden died after a short illness at the age of 80 and Peter Foden, though only 20 at the time, was made a director as it was feared that without the leader figure of E.R. attempts might be made to break the family control of the company. Though very much a junior member, Peter Foden took an active and constructive part in the running of the company, getting involved in many commercial decisions as well as the production aspects and supply problems. There is no doubt at all that E.R. was sorely missed, not only for his acute business brain but also for his friendly attitude to the staff and his sense of humour. That sense of humour was stretched to the utmost one day, just after the war, when E.R., who had bought an ex-airforce tractor to move chassis around the works, asked Peter to take a photograph of him driving it. Peter Foden recounts the tale with a certain degree of relish. His father drove the tractor round the yard, then straight towards his son. Determined to get a close up shot, Peter stood his ground, and determined to frighten him E.R. drove straight at him. At the last instant Peter leapt aside, photo safely in the camera. To his horror E.R. realised he was heading for a new chassis awaiting delivery and despite desperate avoiding action there was a crunching and splintering noise. One more candidate for ERFs efficient repair shop was entered in the books. However, such pranks were not the normal behaviour at Sandbach and even in the difficult years of the 1940s the company made a steady profit.

Sad though the passing of E.R. Foden was, there was nothing to be gained by looking back. With the company thoroughly established as a major truck builder with production approaching the prewar peak, plans were made for the future. These were made without the immediate help of Peter Foden, who was doing two years compulsory service in the Army in 1953-55, when he served as an officer in the Corps of Royal Electrical and Mechanical Engineers. On his return production was still modest though growing annually. He was made export director and deputy managing director with Dennis as managing director, which of course he had been for many years with his father as chairman. The export trade steadily increased, as did the home market, but competition was increasing not only from other British makers but from overseas too, notably from Germany.

Like his father, Peter Foden had a flair for design and on his return to the company he suggested a new cab design was needed. Sketches based on an astonishingly simple concept, a radius of 8 feet for the profile of the front panel, led to an interim coachbuilt cab with a small oval grille similar to the company logo which soon led to ERF's first glass fibre cab. In 1956 when the KV cab, as it was called, first appeared its spectacular and pure lines took the truck world by storm, and over 20 years later many of those models are still working and still looking as stylish as they did in 1956.

Up to that date, every ERF built with the exception of some wartime hybrids, had been Gardner engined, and very satisfactory they had been too. But as production grew at Sandbach the Gardner supply situation became more difficult. At the same time certain export requirements suggested that alternative engines might be needed. So in 1958 a major policy decision was taken to offer engines other than Gardners in ERF chassis. Purists grumbled as they usually do under such circumstances and what amounted to a rush to the door of Sun Works resulted as various engine makers called to see what, if anything, was in the decision for them. The first Cummins engined truck was a KV-cab eight wheeler, which was delivered to Charles Butts of Northampton in 1958. It was a major milestone, but despite that relatively few non-Gardner ERFs were built until some years later. Another bitter blow fell in 1960 when Dennis Foden died quite suddenly, aged only 60. If anything Dennis was missed even more than his father, for although E.R.'s status gave the company respectability, it was Dennis' energy that made it work. The first era of the company was at an end and things would never be the same again.

Above right Despite war work, trucks were still produced during hostilities to keep industry going, but only by special government permit. The vehicles were very similar to prewar 12 tonners, but with no plating on the radiators, small headlamps and utility bodywork. Note the Ministry of War Transport marking on the cab sides.

Right War time activities involved the production of trucks mainly for the Royal Army Service Corps, based on the successful 12 ton gross civilian model. Some versions were produced with deep water wading equipment preparatory to the Normandy landings in 1944.

WAR AND PEACE

30

ERF

To all Customers and Agents we send the Ministry's deepest gratitude for this magnificent gift to our Nation

ERF

The World's Best Oil-Engined Lorries

E.R.F. LTD. SUN WORKS. SANDBACH. CHES.
Directors, E. R. FODEN & DENNIS FODEN
Telephone: Sandbach 225 Telegrams: ERF Sandbach

WAR AND PEACE

Right and below right During the war ERF ran a raffle at £5 a ticket for this DE4 truck in order to buy a Spitfire fighter. The total of over £5000 was quickly raised by dealers and operators and the proceeds sent to the Ministry of Aircraft Production. The plane went into service with a Canadian squadron.

Left The company made suitable and justified publicity out of their purchase of a Spitfire, in addition to their other contributions to the war effort. The letter to Lieutenant Colonel Moore-Brabazon asks for the aircraft to be called 'ERF', but it was in fact christened 'Sun Works'.

Below A batch of 12 military CI5s at the factory prior to delivery in 1941. Apart from oddments like gas indicators, radiator guards, special lighting and camouflage paint, they are little different from civilian trucks.

Left Easy does it! An ageing ERF CI5 helps Britain into the jet age, transporting the revolutionary AW-52 'flying wing' experimental aircraft from the Armstrong Whitworth factory at Baginton, Coventry to Boscombe Down airfield, Hampshire, where its flight trials took place. This advanced aircraft first flew in 1947.

Right The horses outside Bibby's Mills at Liverpool seem to be taking a dim view of a new ballasted tractor in the early mists of a 1949 spring morning. Horses and steam wagons were still common on Merseyside at that time. These ERF tractors replaced aged Foden steamers.

Below right A pair of wartime CI5 tractive units took part in the victory parade in London on June 8th 1946 carrying agricultural equipment used by the Womens Land Army. King George VI and Queen Elizabeth, now the Queen Mother, took the salute accompanied by Queen Mary and the young Princesses, Margaret and Elizabeth, now Queen.

Below Industrial production had to be maintained during the war and this tractive unit, fitted with a double reduction axle, was one of the small number of Gardner-powered units released to non-military users at that time.

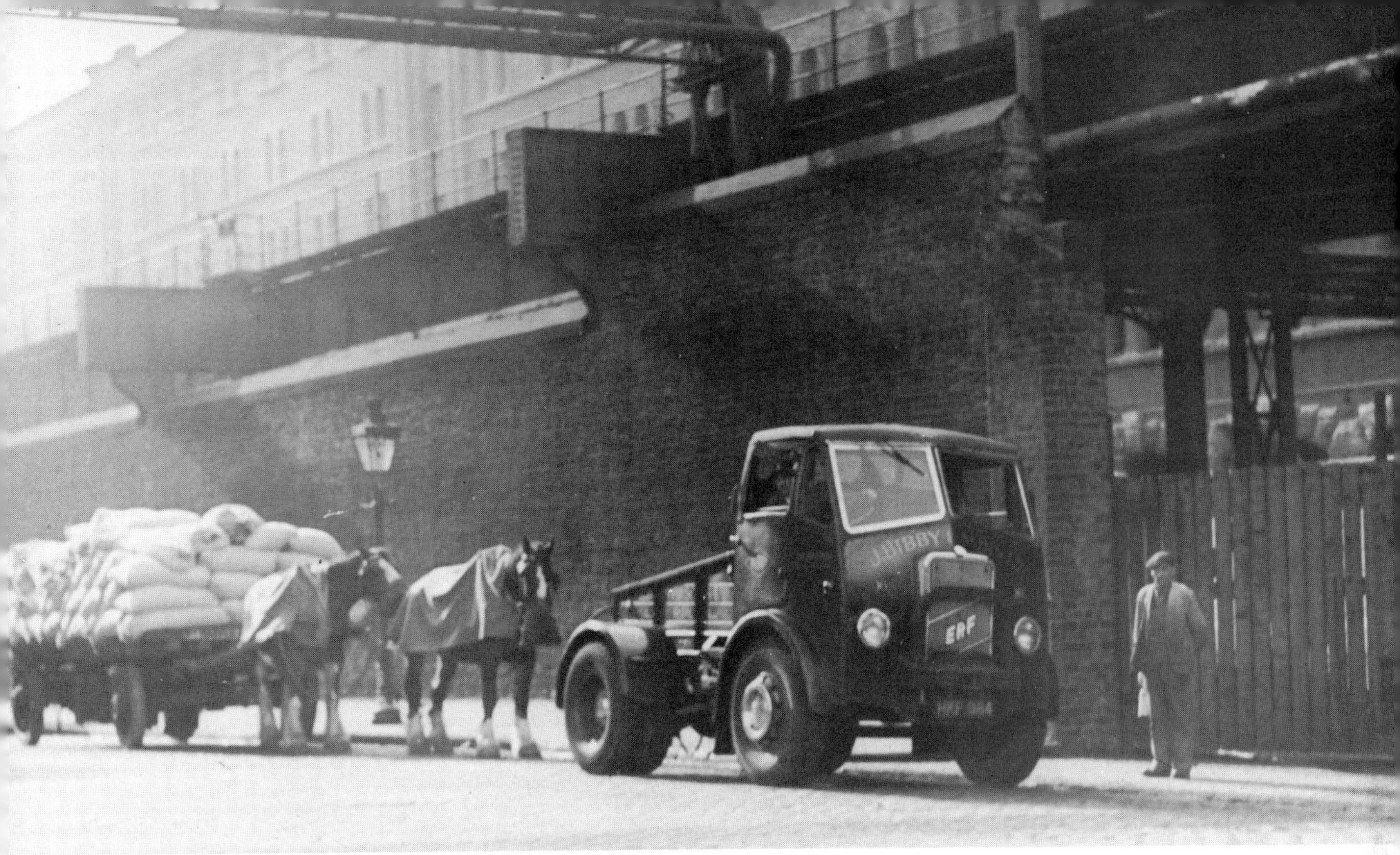
J. BIBBY
ERF

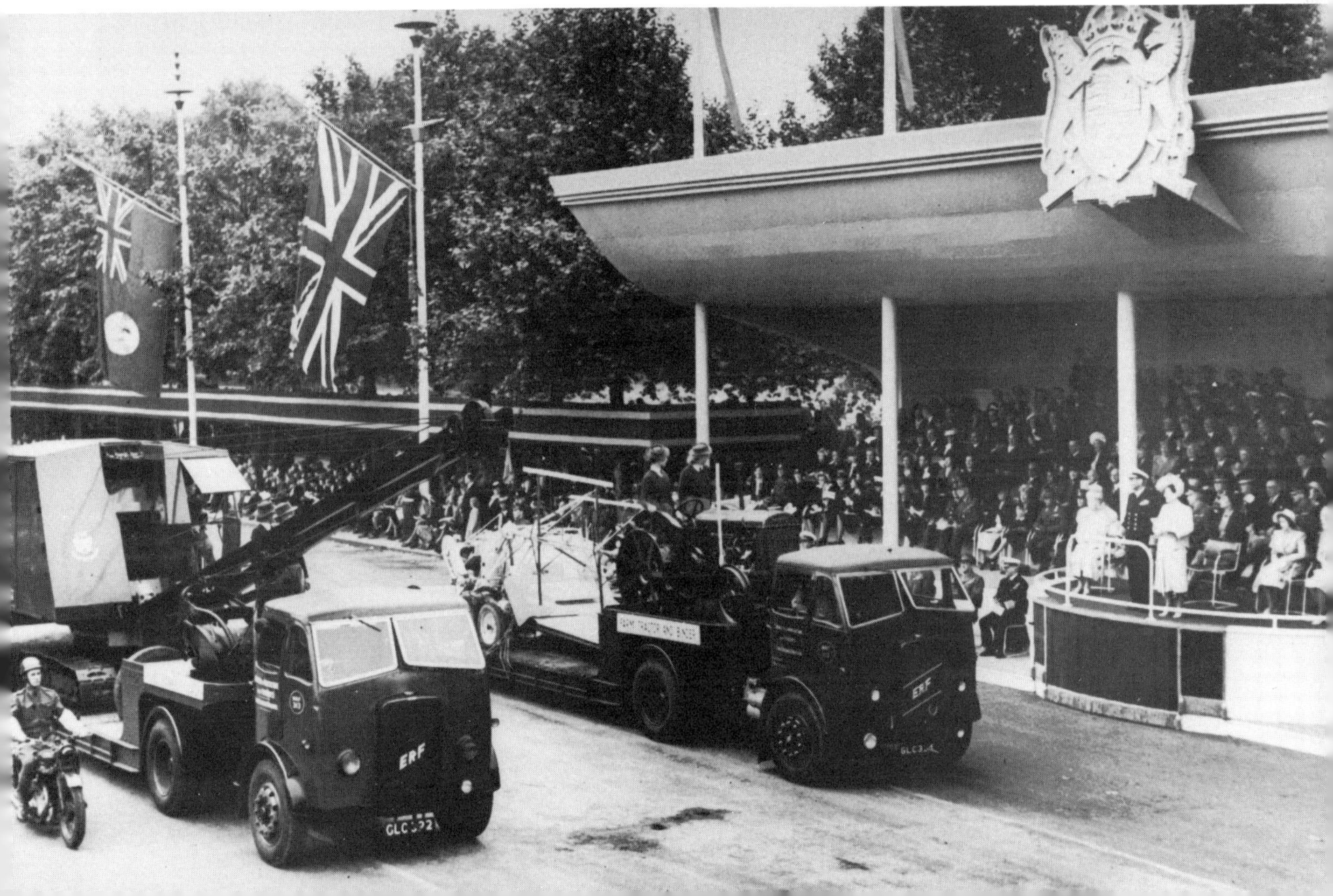
ERF
ERF

Left Drawing of the dash layout for the new postwar models of 1948 shows little advancement over the 1930s. The panel is the standard CAV commercial vehicle set, widely used by Leyland, and used for a short time by ERF. Mechanical controls are strictly in the 1930s style.

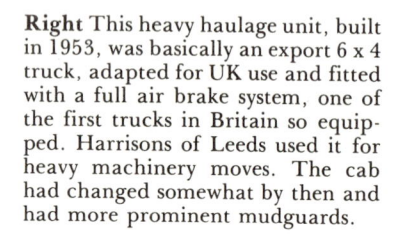

Right This heavy haulage unit, built in 1953, was basically an export 6 x 4 truck, adapted for UK use and fitted with a full air brake system, one of the first trucks in Britain so equipped. Harrisons of Leeds used it for heavy machinery moves. The cab had changed somewhat by then and had more prominent mudguards.

Left First major redesign after the war emerged in the winter of 1947-8 with the so-called 'Streamline' cab. An elaborate curved grille and flush fitting headlamps were supplied already fitted to the front dash plate which formed the cab foundation. Later vehicles had flared sidelights instead of the utility type on this prototype 44 ET model.

Right Quality attracts quality; Rolls Royce at Derby added this Gardner 5LW powered truck to its transport fleet in 1947. That was, of course, before Rolls Royce made automotive diesel engines, which only appeared on the scene some years later. Rolls eventually used ERF chassis as mobile test beds for their own engines.

WAR AND PEACE

Chassis production recommenced after the 1939-45 war with a design very similar to the prewar types. This type C16 chassis was built in 1946 with elaborate showman's tractor bodywork. It had to work hard for its living!

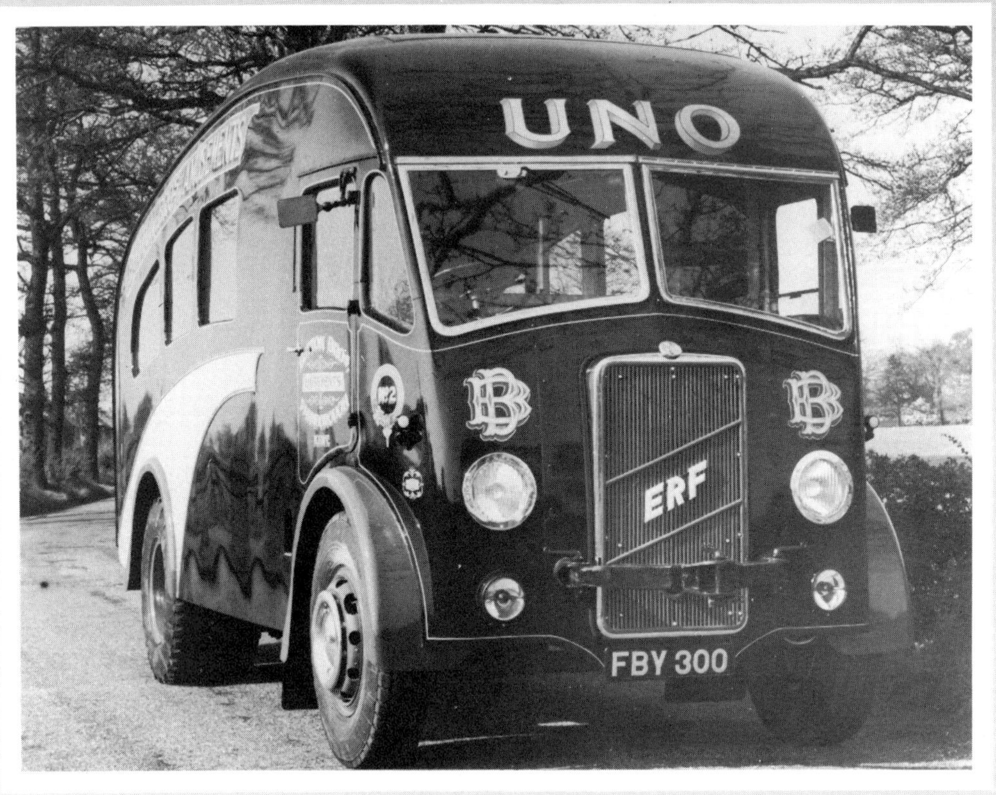
UNO
ERF
FBY 300

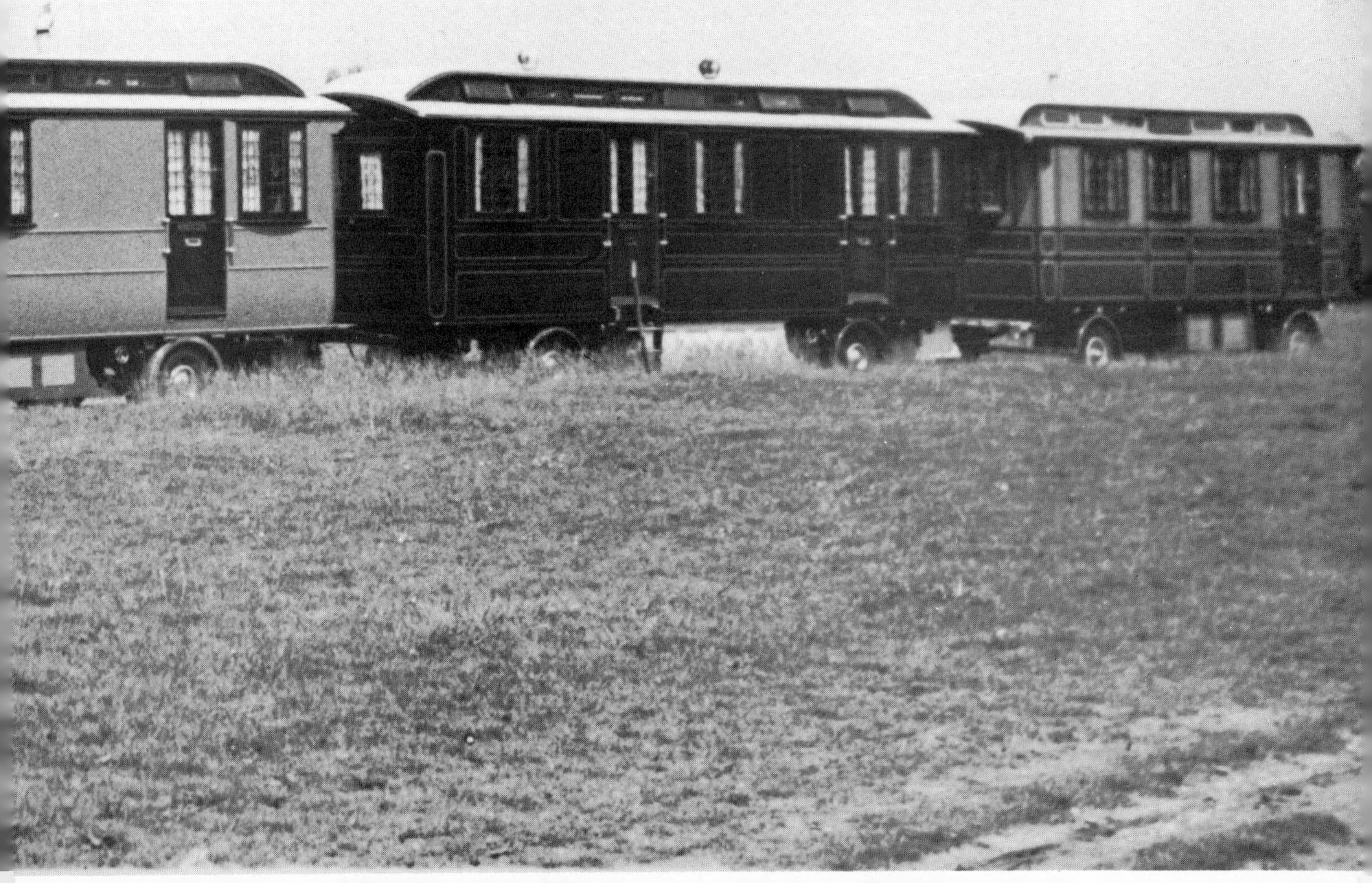

ERF

Left The standard postwar front end styling, with its elegant curved grille, lent itself particularly well to specialist coachwork. ERF supplied the grille and front dash plate, complete with lamps, on to which the body or cab was built. This pantechnicon was built in 1950.

Below The service shop at Sandbach in 1954 contains numerous ERFs both pre- and postwar, a Foden and an ageing Leyland Badger. Good customer service was always an ERF strong point.

WAR AND PEACE

Right This very rare cab was a hybrid version, comprising the 'Streamline' coachbuilt structure, but part-panelled in glass fibre and carrying the oval grille style of the subsequent KV cab. One of these cabs survived to 1977 on a breakdown truck in the Beresford fleet.

Below Very advanced in 1956 and still attractive 20 or more years later, the KV cab design took the British industry by storm when it was introduced. The concept was copied widely but few achieved the purity of line of the original. Many of these models were still working for their living 20 years after manufacture.

Above Engines other than Gardner's began to filter in during the late 1950s. A Rolls Royce diesel was fitted to this 66TS in 1959, probably the first example so fitted.

Background photograph In 1957 a new KV type stands out among four earlier ERFs, half a dozen Sentinels and a Bedford, in the Beresford yard in the Potteries. Note the drivers' long coats in pre-heater days, and the potting kiln, long since demolished.

Above A semi-bonneted version of the KV cab was built to provide three seats for users like brewers, who operated with three man crews. The model was nicknamed 'Sabrina' due to a passing resemblance to a particularly bosomy film and television star of the 1950s, but the models' official designation was the 54GSF.

Overleaf Although the oval emblem appeared on ERF stationery from the earliest days, it was not until the mid-1950s that it appeared as a grille design. This cab continued in production until almost three years after the subsequent LV cab appeared in 1962.

84809 & 88836
BERESFORD
TRANSPORT LTD
H.&R. JOHNSON LTD
BERESFORD'S TRANSPORT LTD
TUNSTALL, STOKE-ON-TRENT
BERESFORD TRANSPORT LTD HIGH ST TUNSTALL STOKE-ON-TRENT
ERF
UEH 664

INNOVATION AND EXPANSION

After Dennis Foden died, Peter Foden to use his own words 'claimed the job as managing director, as there seemed to be a vacant chair and nobody around to fill it.' The company had been reformed as a public company in 1953 after paying the death duties following E.R. Foden's passing, but control still remained with the family, reinforced by Dennis' son Tim, who joined the firm straight from college, and is now a director.

Peter Foden was only 30 years old when he became managing director, and the task facing him would have terrified many able men of that age. The company had been making steady profits, but not developing as well as many would have liked, nor indeed as much as some competitors had done. So Peter brought in new blood. Consultants were engaged to examine market and production matters, new engineers, designers, production and financial brains were grafted into the existing workforce, and options were taken on yet more land for the factory. Chassis designs were developed making them highly competitive without abandoning the constant quality concept started in 1933. And good though the KV cab was, a larger, stronger and more versatile cab design was embarked upon in 1961.

Up to that time all ERF cabs were made by J.H. Jennings right next door in Sandbach, with the exception of those built integrally with special bodywork, a few lightweight Duramin cabs, and those built overseas on export chassis. A young designer called Gerald Broadbent who had worked on the design of the KV cab at Jennings, later joined Boalloy the bodybuilders in nearby Congleton. Jennings' products had got very expensive by that time and some more sensible prices were needed. Broadbent with his cab know-how got a contract to produce a batch of the new LV glass fibre cabs in addition to those that Jennings were to make, a turn of events that did not go down well in the Jennings works, where they considered themselves to have a monopoly of ERF cab production. The direct consequence of that episode came some time later when ERF took over the whole of Jennings' assets and they became part of the ERF group. With the facility of planning and costing their own cab production, and matching it to chassis output, ERF were able to operate a lot more efficiently and production began to expand significantly for the first time since the 1930s.

At the same time there was a major change in the Construction and Use regulations governing the weights and design of trucks in use on British roads. The main change was extending the maximum weight for articulated trucks from 24 tons to 32 tons, while rigid trucks received scarcely any increased weight allowances at all. That was in 1964 and prior to that barely 20 per cent of production had been tractive units for artic operation. However, the change of legislation emphasis meant that within two years 60 per cent of ERF's output was taken up by 30 and 32 ton tractive units, so great was the users' swing to heavy artics. The company had forecast just such a swing, where others had underestimated the popularity of the 32 ton market, and ERF was ready when the orders came flooding in. That big upsurge in output meant that the previously taken decision to offer alternative engines really had to be put into practice. The American manufacturer Cummins was by then producing in-line diesels in Scotland from 170 horsepower upwards, and Rolls Royce were producing their new C-type diesels, later called Eagles, at their plant in Shrewsbury which had once been the home of Sentinel steam wagons. Some lighter chassis had Perkins engines too. With production around the 800-plus chassis a year mark and still increasing, considerable numbers were built with these new engines and that policy has continued ever since although Gardner engines remain a popular choice. In 1977 Gardner were taken over by Hawker Siddeley and this undoubtedly guarantees the continued existence of the company. At around the same time Eaton axles and bogies became common fitments. Eaton units had been used occasionally since the early 1950s, but Kirkstall had still been the major axle suppliers.

With the new range well established and turnover steadily increasing, there was a need to ensure that every possible avenue of technology was explored in keeping ERF in the forefront of truck design. Although the company still assembled their trucks from components supplied from outside—directly opposing the policy of neighbouring Fodens Ltd who at that time made as much as possible themselves—it was necessary to devote a lot of time and money to research to make sure that the right components were doing the right jobs. Consequently throughout the 1960s and the 1970s we find new ideas appearing on ERFs and numerous instances where the company led the British industry into the use of new technology.

There was one specialised, almost revolutionary design built in conjunction with Thomas Hedley in the late 1950s. It was an eight-wheeled tanker chassis designed for liquids deliveries in areas where minimum intrusion was needed, like hospitals and the Houses of Parliament. As a total design it was unsuccessful and only a handful were built, but it bristled with ideas and formed an engineering test bed for much future development. Its engine was a Rolls Royce B81 petrol engine, very smooth and very powerful, giving the laden truck a top speed of a rather illegal 80 mph or more. Disc brakes were fitted which worked well but had short life, Hendrickson rubber suspension showed some promise, and extensive use of alloys, including an all-alloy cab, reduced the weight to under 5 tons complete which was an unprecedented figure for such a chassis. Although many of the lessons from that design taught what should not, rather than what should be done, a great deal of detailed engineering expertise resulted. Perhaps more importantly it gave ERF's engineers a taste of and skill in doing their own research, particularly in brakes and suspension.

With motorways spreading throughout England, brakes became a major source of criticism in the industry. For years it had been accustomed to 20 or 30 mph speed limits and now it was suddenly faced with double those speeds on the motorways. ERF tackled the problem. They were the first truck manufacturers in Britain to fit the two-leading shoe type Stopmaster brake, made by Rockwell in America and built under licence in Britain by Centrax Gears. In fact Centrax never went into full production with them so they had to be dropped eventually, but the episode brought many benefits in good braking techniques. Towards the end of the 1960s the spring brake concept that had been developed by MGM in America was picked up by Ernest Sherratt during an American tour, and he was impressed. At the time the regulations did not allow the use of 'stored energy', ie, springs in brake systems which applied the brakes when the air system failed. However, the spring brake was so attractive both in its 'fail safe' characteristic and its ability to simplify the maze of air piping that was necessary at the time that ERF approached the Ministry of Transport to try 50 sets of the new equipment. The Ministry agreed, and since then the spring brake has become standard equipment not only on ERFs but on virtually every other make of heavy truck. Some only got round to it ten years after ERF, but there is no doubt that it was ERF's initiative that brought about that particular revolution. Another trend led by ERF was the use of the Fuller Roadranger gearbox, eventually to become virtually the standard transmission in UK heavy trucks.

In the early 1970s the typical British truck, ERF included, handled and braked better than any others in the world, but with short stiff springs the ride was dreadful on any but the best road surfaces. In 1969 an entirely new and advanced chassis design was conceived under the engineering leadership of Alan Turner. Ernest Sherratt had by then retired from engineering although he is still a member of the board of ERF (Holdings) Ltd, and a consulting engineer.

Chassis had been getting heavier, more expensive, but not necessarily much better than their predecessors in the view of the directors, not to mention the customers, so a complete re-think was necessary. The result was the A-series models, introduced at the 1972 London show at Earls Court. That design took the industry almost as much by surprise as had the original CI4 model nearly 30 years previously. Gone were the typical short stiff springs and in their place were long flat springs and big dampers that combined good ride with excellent stability.

Chassis hardware like air tanks were built as rationalised groups common to all chassis instead of being added on piecemeal, while frame and crossmember design broke new ground in low weight and great strength. Hydraulic power steering was standard, while power came from Cummins or Gardner engines, including Gardners' new 240 horsepower 8LXB type. A-series chassis were made as tractive units with two or three axles, and haulage trucks on two or three axles, but the eight wheelers continued to be built to the old design. The LV cab continued too, in a restyled form with much improved interior appointments and more sound insulation between engine and driver. In per-

INNOVATION AND EXPANSION

formance, handling and safety the A-series put ERF ahead of all its domestic competitors, although the growing tide of imported trucks in Britain was posing an ever greater threat. It was so popular with truck operators that over 2000 a year were built.

With a whole range of new and up-to-date engineering tried and proven in the A-series, it was high time the cab was brought up to date as well, and in 1974 the B-series made its bow. Chassis engineering was based on the A-series with some changes like the chassis frame width which was reduced to 37 inches from 40 inches, mainly to accept the large 12.00 section tyres demanded in some applications. Chief engineer by this time was Jack Cooke who had joined ERF when his old firm Atkinson was merged with Seddon. Externally the B-series was strikingly handsome with a thoroughly modern cab, fully equipped and furnished to the highest standards. But it was more than just attractive. The structure of the new cab, called the SP type, was a massive steel frame on to which were fitted panels made by hot-moulding plastic resins reinforced by chopped glass fibre. These panels are chemically similar to the common glass fibre or grp, but mechanically very much stronger. In the very severe impact tests carried out at the Motor Industry Research Association under rules laid down by the Economic Commission for Europe, the SP cab emerged with little visible damage apart from broken glass and became the first British cab to meet the standard.

First production B-series trucks were all eight wheelers because there had been no A-series models in that configuration and by March 1975 they were in full production. Two tractive unit prototypes had been built, but those apart, production of B tractive units did not get under way until the middle of 1975. The tooling costs for setting up the B-series production lines, coupled with the slower production during the model changeover, and compounded by a serious economic recession which affected Britain as well as most other industrial nations, produced the very first trading loss in company history in the first half of 1975-76. This was not quite recovered in the second half, making a loss on the year of £118,000. Pundits forecast the downfall of ERF at that point, but those who knew better ignored them and the following year a resounding £1.7 million profit emerged.

In 1977 an exporter sleeper cab version was added to the B-series range, replacing the modified Motor Panels steel cab that had been the main export offering, and that marked a further stage in the planned rationalisation of the entire product range to the basic B-series specification. At the time of writing the annual production figures look like reaching an all-time high of around 3000 chassis, and it is Peter Foden's declared aim to be boss of Britain's number one heavy truck producer, a goal which is very close now. What is significant is that those production figures have been achieved by a family-controlled independent company in competition with international giants, and the standard of engineering technology, safety and aesthetics compares favourably with the best in Europe.

* * *

The export business had formed an important part of the company's activites almost from the start of its operations. The sales ledger records chassis built for various municipalities like Krugersdorp, and Pretoria, as early as the winter of 1934-5 and from then on a steadily increasing stream of vehicles went overseas as their reputation for rugged reliability spread.

South Africa has always been a prime export market, indeed the 1977 annual report shows almost 11 per cent of the company turnover, and no less than 22.3 per cent of the profit coming from that market. ERF was fortunate in having a first class energetic representative in the shape of Trucks and Transport Equipment (Pty) Ltd, in the formative years, and for many years after the Second World War too, when business and reputation was steadily strengthened. In 1964 ERF formed its own company called ERF South Africa (Pty) Ltd, with the object of assembling and marketing chassis that were specially designed for that particularly tough truck market. That the venture was an eventual success can be judged by its contribution to the 1977 trading figures already mentioned. Originally the simple sturdy CI4 and CI5 chassis formed the mainstay of the trade, and even a few of the lightweight OE4 and LK4 chassis went abroad mainly for private companies. But they all had Gardner engines, and they played no small part in the success of the export trade.

But although South Africa can legitimately be called ERF's number one export market, there are others that cannot be overlooked. Since the mid-1960s, the Middle Eastern countries have between them formed a major ERF market. That area is collectively the world's largest single industrial expansion zone and is likely to continue as such into the 1990s. Consequently there is a big need for heavy trucks and ERF found success in its efforts there. Some orders, like the Jordan Phosphates Mines contract for 50 heavy articulated dumpers, were spectacular, but most of them were and are in small quantities. New Zealand is an increasingly important market too, which produced almost 3 per cent of the turnover in 1976-7. That is a particularly difficult market with traffic controls and legislation that are irksome in the extreme. However, ERF found a secure niche there and the business in New Zealand has expanded steadily during the 1970s.

Continental Europe is a highly sophisticated and specialised market, with its own strong domestic truck manufacturing industry. Nevertheless in the mid-1960s ERF took the decision to enter selected continental markets and set about finding suitable dealers and distributors in those areas. The venture was never expected to produce spectacular results against the might of the home manufacturers, but nevertheless a considerable number of ERFs can be seen on the roads of France, Benelux and Switzerland in liveries of local operators. To support those users, a service network was established extending along the main TIR routes towards the Middle East, and extending down to Italy and Spain as well. With the advent of the B-series European sleeper cab trucks in 1977, the model range became technically very competitive. Throughout the 1970s the continental truck markets were severely depressed, far worse in fact than in Britain itself. Under those circumstances spectacular penetration is not possible. Nevertheless, a steady stream of European chassis were and are exported and ERF remains the only British heavy truck manufacturer to sell top-weight chassis on the continent in any appreciable numbers.

In the late 1970s export business accounted for something like 17 per cent of the group turnover and the policy is to hold that figure or perhaps increase it slightly, remembering that steady production increases boost the total in terms of actual numbers, as distinct from percentages.

Above right On its way to Earls Court in 1962 for the first showing of the LV cab models, this 16 tonner bears the legend 'Built for Britain's Motorways' on the sign on its alloy body.

Right Peter Foden, who has headed ERF since 1960.

Above far right The immediate prewar production peak level was not regained until the mid-1950s after steel rationing ended. Major expansion resulted after the re-organisation initiated by Peter Foden from 1961 onwards.

Far right From 1961, when Peter Foden took over as managing director and did some reorganising and introduced this new LV type glass fibre cab, the company was launched into continuous expansion that is still proceeding.

INNOVATION AND EXPANSION 47

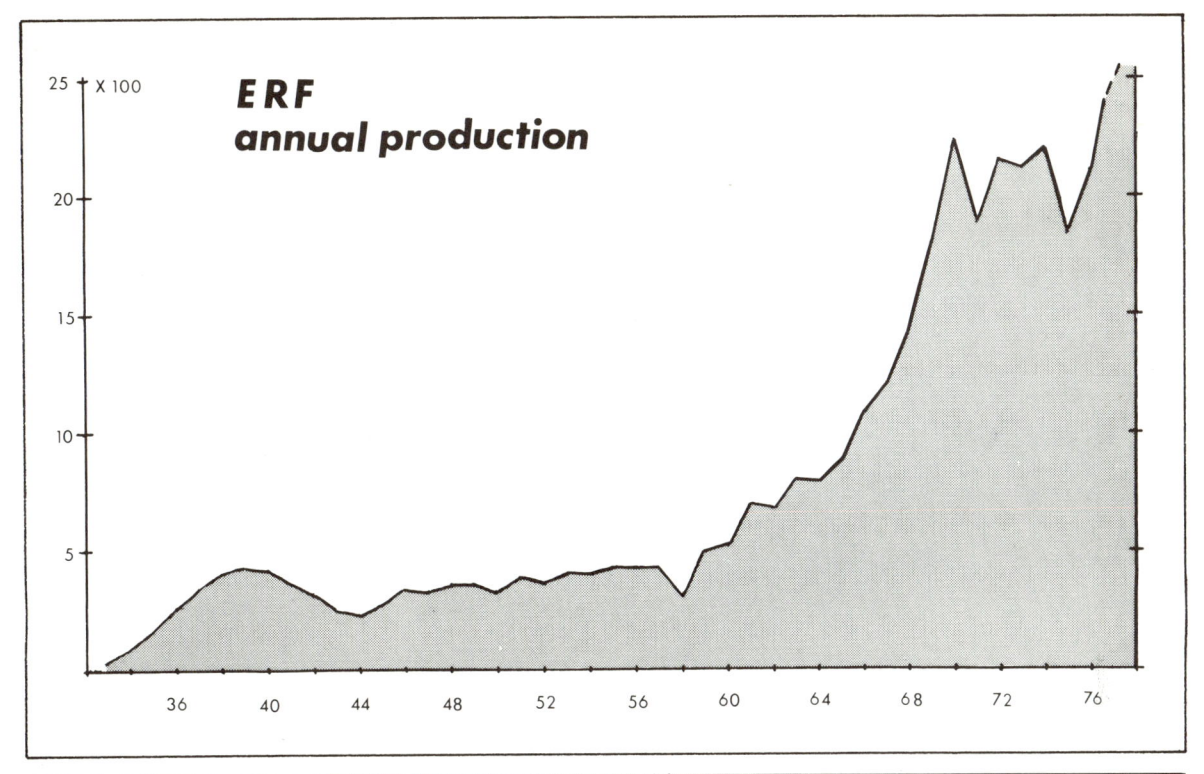

ERF *annual production*

ERF

These pages and overleaf The LV series cab underwent periodic frontal restyling over its 12 year life, culminating in the A-series models which had a surprisingly crisp and clean line. Interiors were steadily improved too, with particular attention to soundproofing.

S&R
490
ERF
LWT 837D
66

EMERTON
ROOFING (WESTERN) LIMITED
HEAD OFFICE
ACTON, NANTWICH
TELEPHONE
NANTWICH 65141
EMERTON
ROOFING CONTRACTORS
ERF
HMA 918G

W. H. GROSE
W.H. GROSE
Haulage Contractors
ST. AUSTELL 3336
WHG
ST. AUSTELL · CORNWALL
ERF
JCV 799L

INNOVATION AND EXPANSION

Below A great deal of engineering know-how went into the lightweight eight wheeler built in conjunction with Shell. It had a Rolls Royce petrol engine, disc brakes and was intended for use in what are now known as 'environmentally sensitive areas'.

ERF

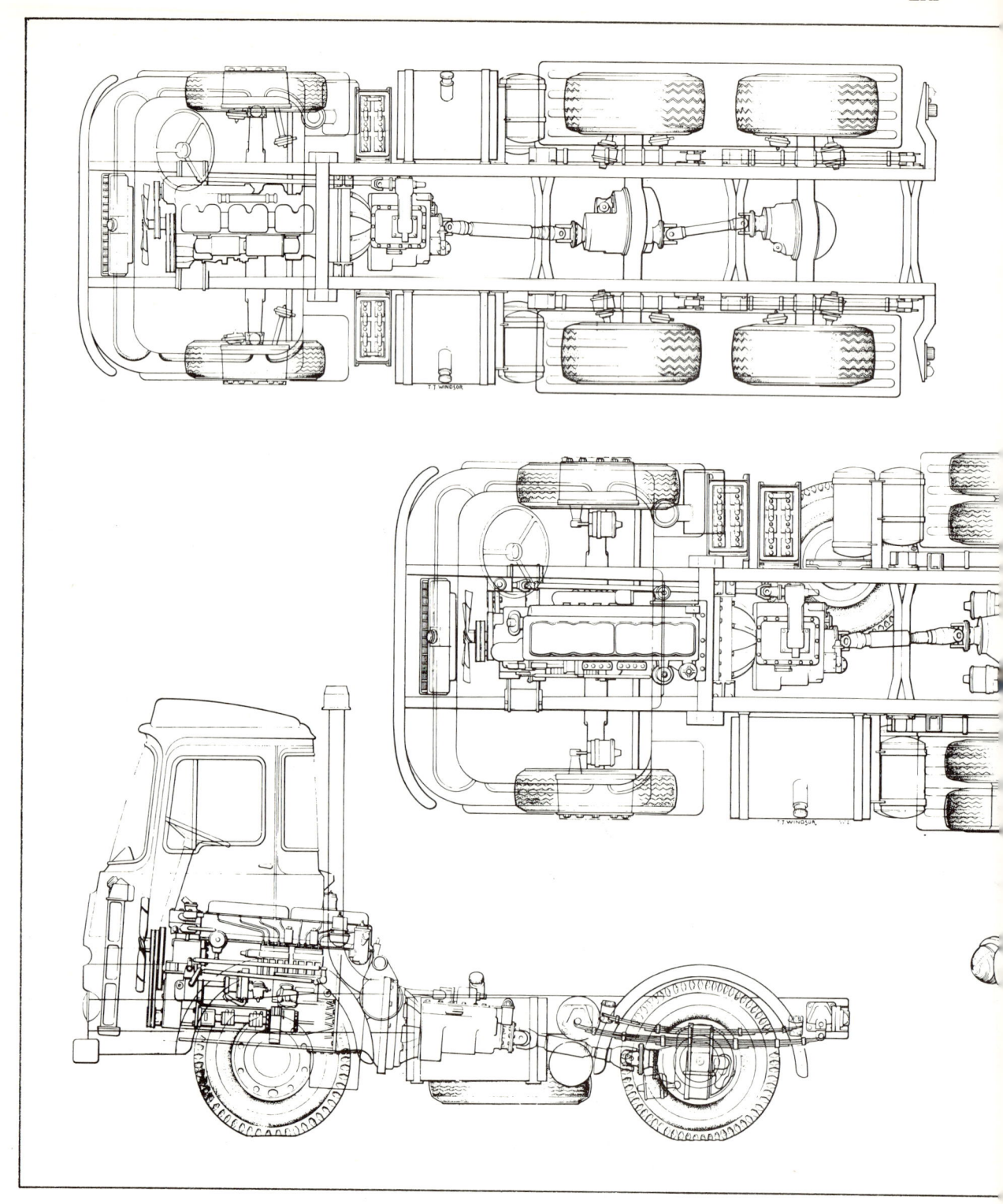

INNOVATION AND EXPANSION 53

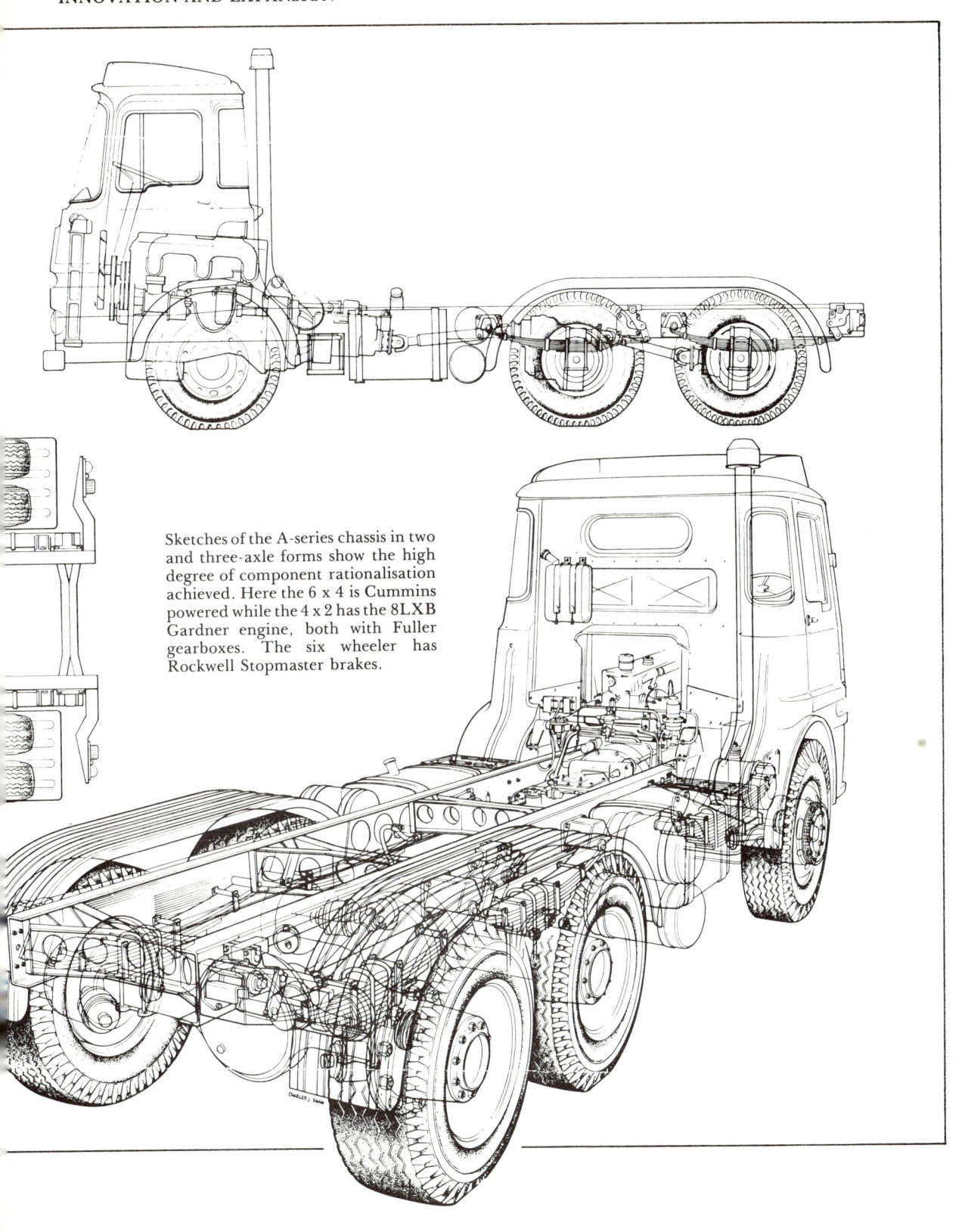

Sketches of the A-series chassis in two and three-axle forms show the high degree of component rationalisation achieved. Here the 6 x 4 is Cummins powered while the 4 x 2 has the 8LXB Gardner engine, both with Fuller gearboxes. The six wheeler has Rockwell Stopmaster brakes.

Left Although there was strong emphasis on the heavy tractive units after the change in UK regulations in 1964, the extremely economical 54G 16 ton four wheeler remained as one of the most popular chassis. A high proportion of them have done well over ten years reliable service for their owners and are still going strong.

Right The A-series models of 1972 represented a big advance in chassis engineering, although a restyled version of the ten year old LV cab was retained. Here, one of the factory machines undergoes high speed stability trials on the Motor Industry Research Association test ground.

Left From 1972 the steel Motor Panels cab was offered as an alternative to the LV glass fibre cab on the home market. The steel cab had already been used for export for some years. This Gardner 240 model joined Russell Cadwallader's fleet at Oswestry.

Right Drawbar trailer work needed sophisticated traffic planning to make the most of its economic potential. Harrisons operated just such a service between Yorkshire and the south with ERF A-64G trucks.

INNOVATION AND EXPANSION

Above and left When the law requiring a mate in the cab of trucks with drawbar trailers was withdrawn in 1972 ERF was quick in providing suitable truck chassis. An A-series chassis powered by a Cummins 220 engine was offered, seen here as it was completed at the works and later during road trials.

Above right ERF was the first user of spring brake units which gave a fail-safe characteristic. That came in useful in this incident where the drive axle lost grip on a slippery hill through the half load in the tank leaving insufficient weight at the front end.

Right One of the first really powerful ERFs sold in Britain was this Cummins 335 horsepower model MKC 852 which went to Kings Plant Haulage Bristol in 1973.

KINGS PLANT HAULAGE
BRISTOL
KINGS PLANT HAULAGE BRISTOL
TEL. BRISTOL 552168
ERF
KING
KINGS PLANT HAULAGE BRISTOL
GHY 129K

Background photograph
Always in the forefront of developments and innovations in the truck industry, ERF was involved with trials of the so called 'double bottom' dual trailer concept in 1973-74, with Crane Fruehauf the trailer builders.

Inset
The first British cab to meet EEC cab strength requirements was ERF's SP, in 1975. This massive weight is swung from a great height into the cab as part of the test.

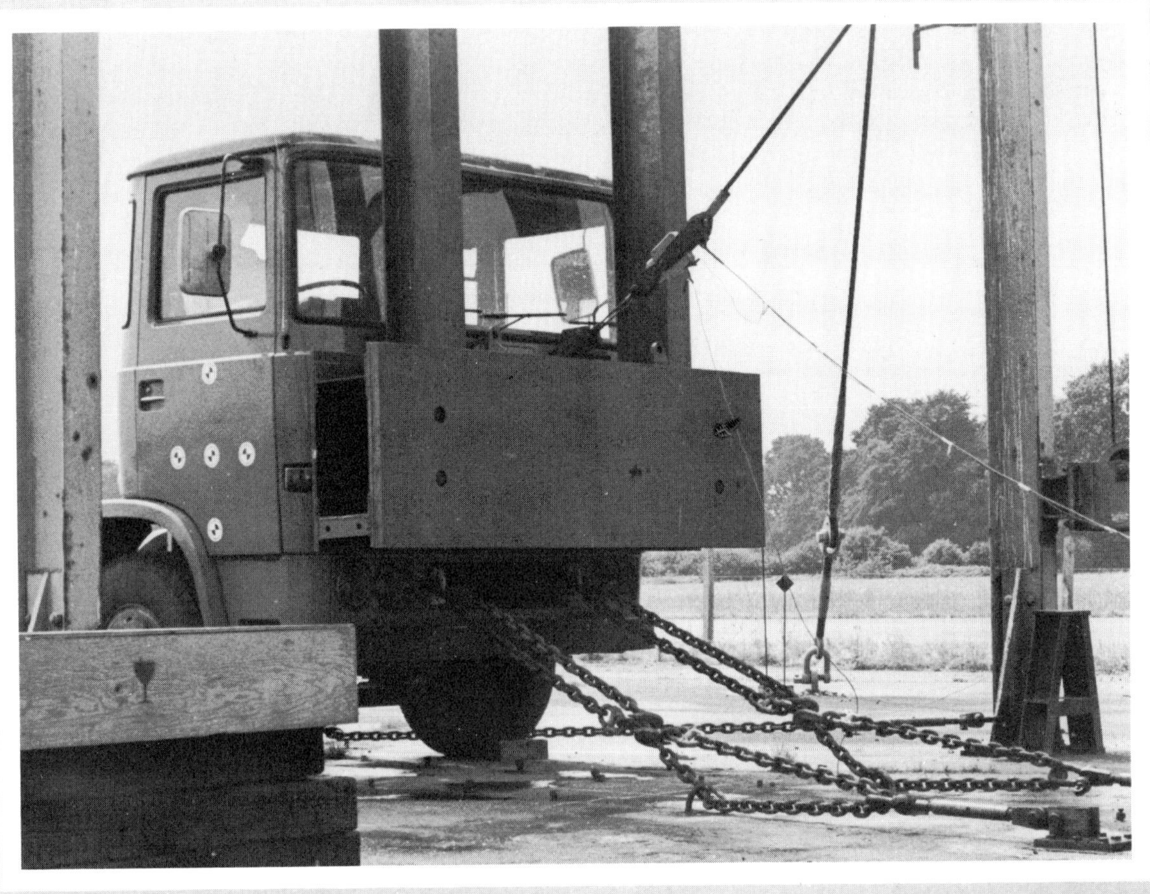

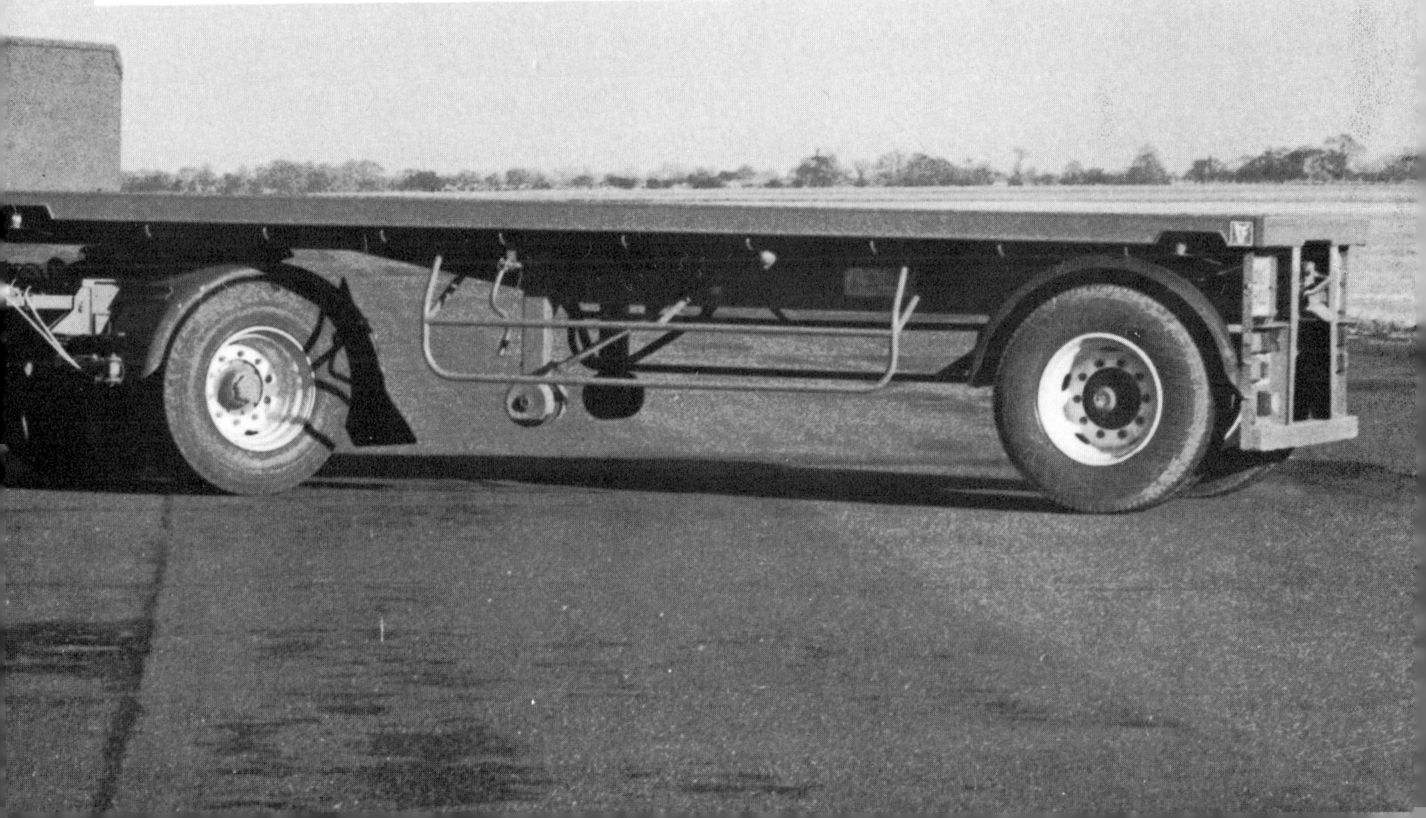

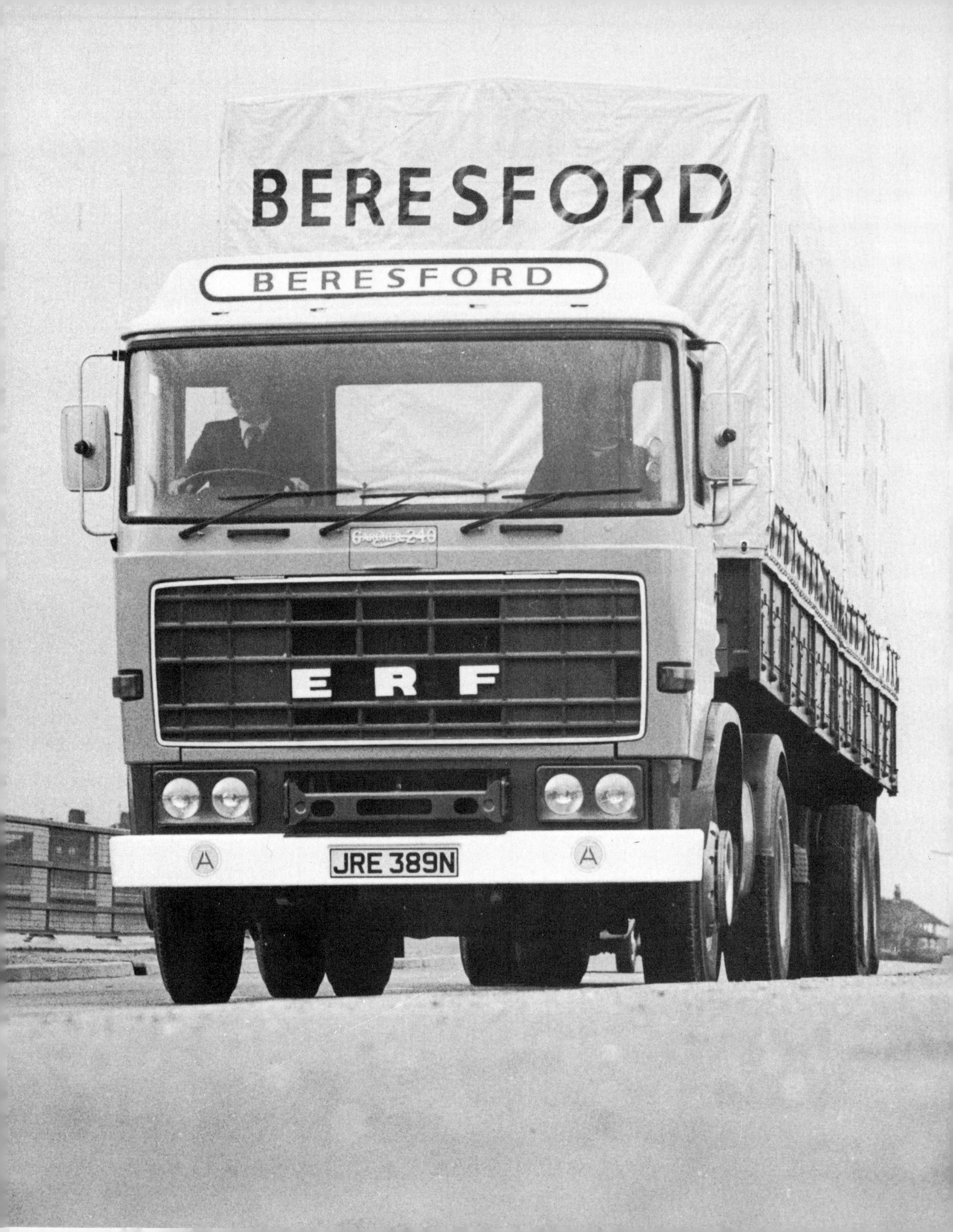
BERESFORD
BERESFORD
ERF
JRE 389N

INNOVATION AND EXPANSION 61

Left and above Star of the 1974 London commercial motor show was the B-series ERF. Two prototypes were shown, one with a Gardner 8LXB engine, which subsequently joined the fleet of long-term ERF users Beresford Transport of Tunstall, Stoke on Trent, in working paint of grey and yellow, as distinct from the orange and chrome of the show finish.

Right Splendid engine access was available on the B-series trucks, the first ERFs to have a tilt cab.

ERF

INNOVATION AND EXPANSION

Above Cab interior of the B-series set new high standards for British trucks in terms of comfort, safety and noise levels.

Above left Dash panel on the B-series is designed round an EEC tachograph and is shaped so that the wheel does not obscure any part of it.

Left Addition of intake stacks behind the cab of the B-series trucks reduced cab noise level by 3dB(A).

Right From the beginning of 1978, multi-axle ERFs became available with a non-reactive bogie, designed to eliminate wheel-hop under braking and generally improve bogie behaviour especially unladen. The tie-rods balance out torque reactions between the axles.

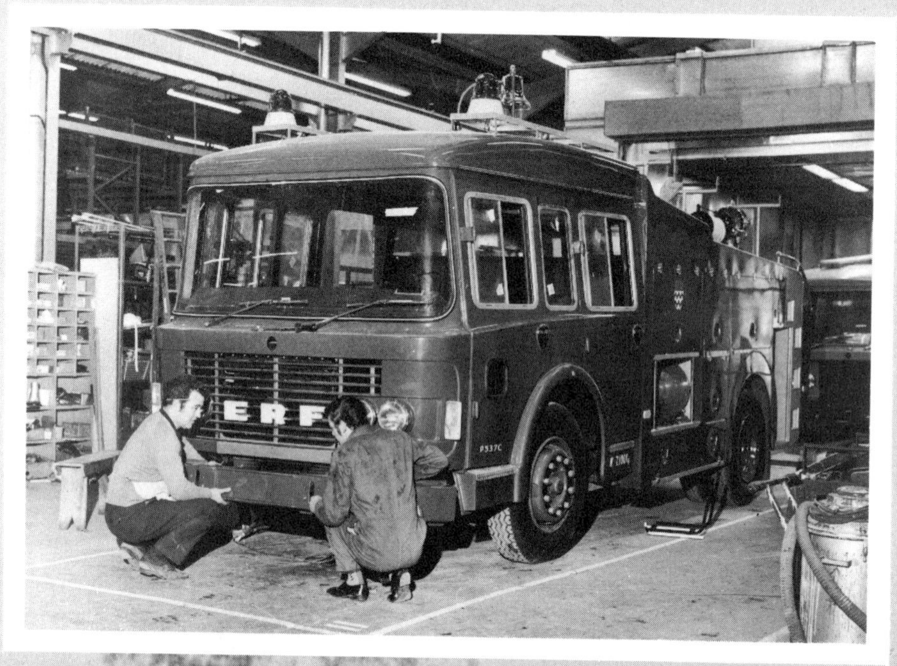
ERF

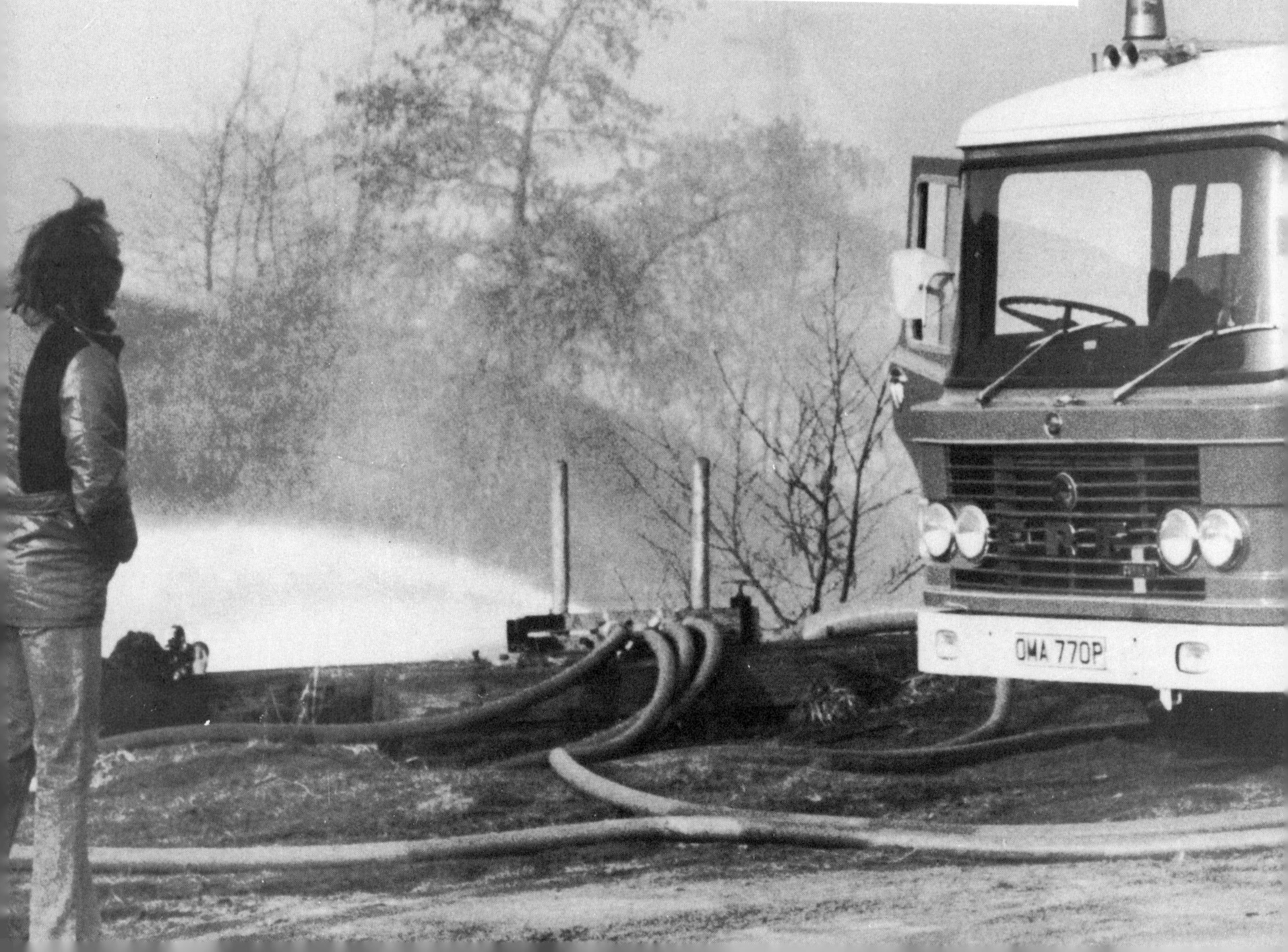
OMA 770P

Inset
Trucks were and are only part of ERF's activity. Fire engines formed a flourishing diversification at a separate factory in Winsford, producing appliances on special ERF chassis and those of other makes. In 1977 that division was renamed Cheshire Fire Engineering Ltd, remaining part of the ERF group.

Background photograph
ERF's very fast and powerful firefighter chassis were equipped with high capacity pumps and advanced equipment like the roof mounted monitor jet and hand-held fog guns. This example is undergoing pumping tests at Winsford.

ERF

Left Before the proper factory sleeper cab was available, Bristol operator Joseph Fish converted the normal cabs to accommodate a folding bunk.

Below, opposite and overleaf Although great emphasis was placed on the tractive unit B-series models at the 1974 London show, it was the eight-wheeled 30 tonner that went into production first. This was because there was no eight wheeler chassis in the A-series range and a new model was long overdue. They were immediately successful in a wide range of application.

STEETLEY
STEETLEY
STEETLEY
ERF
D14

B & J. DAVIES LTD
TIMBER
ERF
LAW 971·P
GARDNER 180

ERF

INNOVATION AND EXPANSION

Below Sleeper version of the B-series cab design incorporated a raised roofline to accommodate two bunks within EEC dimensions. As well as export users, some UK operators like this one, use sleeper Bs for international haulage across Europe.

Above It was nearly two years after the introduction of the B-series models that the factory offered a sleeper cab. In the meantime operators bought proprietary sleeper conversions like this one, built by Jennings Coachworks, Crewe.

Left This CI5 tractor chassis was hauling heavy machines in South Africa on a Tasker low loader long before the Second World War. The cab, though resembling the normal Jennings design, was built locally, with a double skin roof.

INNOVATION AND EXPANSION

Above The 'Chinese-six' 66TS was tried in South Africa but never became popular. The cab and body on this example are locally built based on the normal factory dashplate and grille. The truck operated from an industrial suburb of Johannesburg in 1952.

Right Thatcher Hobson operated ERFs on long distance services in Rhodesia for many years. These two CI5s worked out of Broken Hill carrying passengers freight and mail. Thatcher Hobson had mail contracts which gave rise to the use of post-wagons very similar to those used in Sweden and Norway.

Inset right The South African dealers were Trucks and Transport Equipment (Pty) Ltd, seen here in 1940 with the ever popular CI5 tipper parked outside.

Inset below Scarcely recognisable as ERFs these two tippers covered well over a million miles each, shifting gold mine waste for Roussouw Mine Transportation Corporation in South Africa. They are not derelict as this picture suggests, merely waiting for new drivers at a change of shift when they were photographed in 1973.

Background photograph This heavy machinery transporter working in Natal in 1972 was originally a Cummins engined long wheelbase 6 x 4 truck, but had a 'tag' axle added locally to carry extra weight. The trailer has a hydraulic folding gooseneck.

TRUCKS & TRANSPORT EQUIPMENT
(PTY.) LTD.
ERF
& Bristol
SERVICE
S.J. McILRATH LTD.
S.J. McILRATH LTD.
QUARRY
NATALSE PAAIE DEPT.
NPA. 4776
ERF

One of ERF's more widely publicised export orders was for the Jordan Phosphates Mines Co in 1969. All 50 vehicles were delivered overland with their King hopper trailers, for which purpose they were registered in Britain before starting out. The 6 x 4 heavy duty tractive units had Rolls Royce Eagle engines and spring brakes.

نقليات موارد الأردن
JORDAN PHOSPHATES MINES CO.
JORDAN RESOURCES TRANSPORT
ERF
PDD 220 G

THORNTONS
P.O. BOX 91
WELKOM
ORANGE FREE STATE

Ets THIBAUT
PRODUITS AGRICOLES
6448 STREE
Tel. 071/533085
ERF

INNOVATION AND EXPANSION

Above Surprise exhibit at the 1973 Brussels show was a new 'European' heavy tractive unit, with a striking cab design based on the Motor Panels shell. Engines were 335 horsepower turbocharged Cummins units. This range formed the spearhead of ERF's European operations until 1977, when the B-series versions followed.

Above left Even some 'Sabrina' SFC models found their way overseas. The only 'export' concessions on this one were a sun-shade roof, heavy duty wheels and tyres, and higher than usual ground clearance. It went to work as a tipper in the Orange Free State.

Left The long-wheelbase 'European' was rated at 42 tonnes when hauling a drawbar trailer, which this Belgian user seems to have left behind on this occasion.

Right One of the features of the European range is an outstanding roadholding characteristic. Only the tyre deflection betrays the fact that this truck is cornering at nearly 50 mph fully laden.

Right Hauling loads up to 300 tonnes, in this case 'double heading' with another tractor, a special bonneted chassis with ballast box was built to move sections of a new oil refinery in South Africa in 1971. Power was by Cummins and a Motor Panels cab was incorporated in the rather basic superstructure.

Below Despite a compact wheelbase of only 3.2m the ERF European tractive unit could hitch a wide variety of semi-trailers including the 1.6m overhang type popular in continental haulage. These 335 horsepower turbocharged Cummins powered machines had a very high performance at 38 tonnes.

INNOVATION AND EXPANSION

SERVICE AND SUCCESS

Throughout the development of ERF as a company, close liaison was maintained with the truck-user customers as a matter of basic policy, as it was believed that in this way the product could be kept fully up to date, and new ideas could be blended into the vehicle designs in a thoroughly practical manner. In general that policy worked although it was not without its abrasive moments from time to time.

In prewar days the addition of five speed gearboxes as an option to the normal four speed unit was a direct result of user consultation, and indeed the development of the heavy duty six-wheeled and eight-wheeled chassis, which were the first to have five gears, took place in close cooperation with hauliers who foresaw the need for them. Despite the use of higher powered five and six cylinder engines the hill performance required was not forthcoming with the four speed gear box, especially when towing loaded trailers across Britain's hilly northern regions and that extra ratio was vital. At that same period larger fuel tanks were also offered because hauliers needed to make long round trips without refuelling at the relatively expensive roadside diesel fuel pumps, making full use of the bulk discount prices that were beginning to be available to truck operators.

In postwar years, as truck technology became more advanced and complex, user involvement became more intense. For example the 64P ultra-light-weight concrete mixer chassis built in 1968 for Tyneside concrete contractors, Gibson Readymix, was a result of close user-manufacturer cooperation. Gibsons needed a compact four-wheeled mixer for urban building sites that would carry a full five cubic yard load of wet concrete mix, which meant a nine ton payload. Not only did it have to be light, but very tough too, and numerous innovations appeared in that machine which marked the beginnings of new design trends. Big 'super-single' rear tyres were fitted, so were two-leading shoe Rockwell brakes. Various items of chassis hardware in aluminium or plastics helped to reduce weight and the whole chassis complete weighed under four tons. Automatic brake adjusters were also pioneered on this chassis.

Relations with progressive thinking operators were not always smooth however, even if the results usually paid off in the end. Although ERF's long-used vacuum-hydraulic brake system was among the best available in the 1930s, by the late 1940s and early 1950s they were less than inspiring in their performance, despite the addition of air servos rather than vacuum equipment. Having seen Westinghouse air brake systems on foreign trucks, and experienced Clayton air systems on Sentinels, Bert Middleton, the fleet engineer of Beresford Transport in the Potteries, asked ERF to fit air brakes. Beresfords experienced severe brake problems, especially on their hilly routes from the Midlands to Liverpool and Manchester. It seems that Dennis Foden was less than enthusiastic, politely asking Mr Middleton to go away because 'We know more about brakes than you do. . . .' But Bert Middleton finally made his point and in 1958 two new six wheelers were fitted with Westinghouse air brakes for Beresfords, like some export models.

Beresfords were not the only ones complaining about brakes at that time. One of the very first ERF customers, George Baker and Son in Southampton, who are still ERF users today, had been badgering the factory to adopt air brakes. The crunch came, literally, when George's son Eric contrived to have an accident right inside ERF's factory with a truck on which he had been having brake problems and brought back to the works for discussion, and hopefully some action too. Nobody is quite sure whether the accident was really such, or whether there was a bit of desperation involved, but it helped to do the trick and Eric Baker got his air brakes. Shortly afterwards, air brakes were adopted as standard on all heavy ERF chassis.

SERVICE AND SUCCESS

The Baker family business certainly had more contact than most with ERF, and they are probably the longest continuous users of ERFs in existence. It was George Baker who persuaded the factory to build him a tractive unit for low-loader work in 1934, the first to be built. It subsequently became a standard model and was added to the catalogue. That same low-loader, still working nearly 30 years later, became the cause of frame breakage problems as king pin loads got steadily higher. To affect a cure, 10 inch deep flitched frames were designed in place of the original 8 inch frames, originally for Bakers and then as a production item. Bakers also had their early heavy tractors fitted experimentally with auxiliary reduction gearboxes, to spread the total performance range, and that too became a listed option. Eric Baker summed up the point neatly in his own words, 'Whatever the problems, they would always listen to you at ERF. They didn't always agree, but at least they listened and that was more than most factories would.'

A unique position among ERF's customers is occupied by L. Gardner & Sons the engine manufacturers, as they were also suppliers of course. In prewar years they had some very smart 12 tonners with very elaborate special coach built cab and body designs, but it was the installation of the engines, and the detailed technology that went with them that was probably the major contribution. Such matters as exhaust characteristics, inlet manifold and filter depression, all contributed towards the economy and efficiency factors, as well as the basic engines themselves. Gardner are still ERF users and suppliers today. Among their fleet they have two 20-year-old LK model 9 tonners, each with nearly 500,000 miles to their credit, neither of which has required a major mechanical overhaul. One delivers parts and engines to user factories, the other runs to dealers and operators all over Britain. When one considers that both these trucks have a life-long fuel consumption record of more than 24 mpg, or less than 11.5 litres per 100 km, one wonders if some manufacturers have lost their way somehow in more recent years in the light of that performance.

In order to reach the £38.4 million turnover and £1.7 million profit achieved in 1977, which apart from the 1976 loss already explained had represented a steady build up of business since 1961, major changes in the company organisation had to be made. First of all the repair and service shop, so necessary to look after customers' problems once the trucks were in service, was moved out of the main works in Sandbach in 1971 to a completely new and spacious works in the nearby town of Middlewich. The space so vacated left more production room at Sun Works, so enabling the rapidly increasing production of the 1960s and 1970s to continue.

Shortly afterwards the fire engine building activity, which had also been done at the main plant, was moved to a new factory at Winsford, about ten miles away, to continue trading as ERF Fire Engineering Ltd, again making more room for the main chassis production. In 1977 the fire company was renamed Cheshire Fire Engineering, reflecting the restricted local authority budgets which led to them being forced to purchase cheaper fire engines on proprietary truck chassis, rather than the purpose-built but expensive ERF fire chassis. Nevertheless, the fire engine activity contributed about £2.7 million to the turnover in 1977, and continues to grow. Meanwhile production of truck chassis continued to increase and looked like reaching an all time record of close to 3000 a year as this book went to print.

That steady progression from £220,000 profit from £2.5 million turnover in 1961, to the current figures represents a personal triumph for Peter Foden and his team. Although the rate of inflation has contributed to that in recent years in terms of actual values, it is worth remembering that until 1971 inflation was only 2-3 per cent a year, and in that year profits were £915.000 from a turnover of £12.6 millions. The question is whether that rate of expansion can continue. Within the present premises it clearly cannot go on much further. Production rate in 1977 was 14 chassis a day and the plant's ultimate capacity is 19 to 20 a day and no more. As ERF's production methods rely heavily on know-how and individual skills, and less on elaborate tooling and expensive capital equipment, the costs of setting up new manufacturing plants are less than they would be at most truck plants and this seems a likely event sometime before the end of the decade. The company's borrowings have been consistently low, and raising the modest capital necessary would be, according to Peter Foden, a relatively easy task. New models are already on the drawing boards for probable introduction in 1978-9, while more and more chassis are planned for export. The company's experience has shown that export work can be encouragingly profitable, and consequently is likely to continue.

Back in 1970 ERF was the subject of consideration in a merger with Atkinson, but in the event Atkinson merged with Seddon at Oldham, leaving ERF as a staunch independent producer. A company of that size is inevitably vulnerable to takeover in the economic climate of the 1970s and 1980s, but with shareholders so fiercely loyal as ERF's have shown themselves to be, coupled with the company's strong position in home and export markets, it would have to be a very powerful bid indeed that would cause ERF to lose its independence, and under current conditions it must be considered unlikely.

In the meantime ERF remains as a major independent force in the trucking business with one of the most competitive and advanced model ranges on the market, and one of the strongest trading positions of all. There can be no doubt about it, both Edwin Richard Foden and his son Dennis Foden, would have approved of the way their company developed. Even in the pressures of the modern age, their original concept has still been maintained and future models now on the drawing board, as well as those in the development stages like the new lightweight compact M-series, still contrive to blend the original concept of 1933 with the complex international legislative requirements of the 1980s. Few trucks have so successfully combined solid tradition with advanced engineering as ERF.

Show finish standards in the 1950s and 1960s were faultless, as illustrated by these trucks in 1960. In the end Beresfords did not take delivery of the truck in their livery on the stand at Earls Court, and both joined the A.H. Davey fleet.

SERVICE AND SUCCESS

Inset below Exhibits for the 1956 motor show included twin steer and eight wheeler KV models in operators colours, and a 6 x 4 tipper chassis. They are seen waiting to enter the Earls Court exhibition building.

Background photograph Air brakes were fitted as standard on ERFs from 1958, following prompting from Staffordshire operators Beresford Transport among others who had steep hills to contend with in everyday service. These two 56G models are doing trials with the new Westinghouse air brakes on Mow Cop hill.

Inset below Chloride batteries use lift trucks to handle the cargo, and these ride on the tail end of the ERF six wheelers when in transit.

Below Believed to be the first two-axle mixer chassis to accommodate 5 cubic yards of wet concrete, this 64P type was specially planned and built to that end in 1968. The specification including Rockwell Stopmaster brakes, alloy mudguards, big single tyres and a single reduction axle, all motivated by a Perkins 6.354 engine.

Right One of the very first ERF users was Bakers Transport, who bought their first ERF at the 1933 motor show. Here the firm transports an early hovercraft in 1958. Mr. Eric Baker with pipe, son of the founder, is riding on the hovercraft.

Below right In 20 years this 9 ton LK4 model covered nearly half a million miles without major overhaul, working in Gardner Engines' own fleet. When this picture was taken in August 1977 it was delivering new Gardner LXB engines to the ERF plant.

SERVICE AND SUCCESS

ERF

Left Few manufacturers can claim to have trucks over 15 years old in regular service in the numbers that ERF have. This 1958 model was just one of seven that passed within 40 minutes of observation on a British motorway in 1977, and it was still clearly earning good revenue.

Below A limited number of twin steer tractive units were built, principally for the 32 ton five axle requirement that was popular under C and U regulations until 1972. Kentish TIR operators, Lowe's of Paddock Wood, used them for European work for many years with sleeper cabs and powered by Cummins engines.